Getting Started with Conjoint Analysis

Strategies for Product Design and Pricing Research

Second Edition

Bryan K. Orme

Research
Publishers
LLC

Getting Started with Conjoint Analysis:
Strategies for Product Design and Pricing Research
Second Edition
by Bryan K. Orme
Copyright © 2010 by Research Publishers LLC

Publisher
Research Publishers LLC
660 John Nolen Drive
Madison, WI 53713–1420
USA
http://www.research-publishers.com

ISBN10 0–9727297–7–1 ISBN13 978–0–9727297–7–2 (full text, paper)
ISBN10 1–60147–110–6 ISBN13 978–1–60147–110–9 (full text, electronic)

Cover art by Paul Klee (1879–1940)
Maske Furcht, 1932, 286 (Y 6)
100 x 57 cm
Ölfarbe auf Jute auf Keilrahmen
The Museum of Modern Art, New York
Copyright © 2005 Artists Rights Society (ARS), New York
VG Bild-Kunst, Bonn
Digital Image © 2005 The Museum of Modern Art
Licensed by SCALA / Art Resource, New York

Cover design by Jane Tenenbaum, Tenenbaum Design, Cambridge, Mass.
Electronic typesetting by Amy Hendrickson, TEXnology, Inc., Boston.
Printed and bound by R. R. Donnelley and Sons, Allentown, Pa.

Printed in the United States of America.   9 8 7 6 5 4 3 2 1

Contents

Appendices

Foreword

Comments on the first edition of *Getting Started with Conjoint Analysis.*

Bryan Orme's book on conjoint analysis promises to be a new and excellent addition to the literature. Currently, virtually every marketing research text provides at least a chapter or so on conjoint analysis. More ambitious academic works include the book by Gustafsson, Herrmann, and Huber (2000) and the monograph by Krieger, Green, and Wind (2005).

Orme's contribution is something else again. Rather than adopt a typical pedantic approach, Orme's book is a practical, no-nonsense guide to what happens when one designs, executes, and analyzes data from real, marketplace problems. It should appeal to academics and consultant-practitioners alike.

An essential feature of the book is its emphasis on specialized software that enables the analyst to implement real-world studies. (I suspect that Sawtooth Software's founder, Rich Johnson, has played a pivotal role in the software department.)

Over a thirty-five-year period, conjoint analysis has grown from a relatively crude approach to a method with a high degree of sophistication. High-profile applications have included the following:

- Design of AT&T's first cellular telephone
- Design and implementation of the EZ-Pass toll collection system
- Development of new varieties of Mama Celeste pizzas
- New logo design for the Baltimore Ravens football team
- U.S. Navy reenlistment benefits
- New services for the Ritz Carlton and Marriott hotel chains

The book is easy to follow, while at the same time being almost encyclopedic in its coverage of topics ranging from study design to the presentation of results to clients.

Different reviewers will probably have their own favorite chapters, a reflection of built-in biases. I particularly liked the chapter that deals with real cases provided by practitioners. This is a fine idea and provides incentives for consultants and company-based researchers to share their experiences regarding methodological (if not substantive) issues.

I also very much appreciated chapter 1, which explains in simple terms the main ideas of conjoint analysis and related techniques. Chapter 5 provides a very nice overview of conjoint method selection. I also liked the "short history of conjoint analysis" chapter describing how things got started and matured through the years.

Chapter 10 is a very important chapter in the book. This is where the application of conjoint simulators and optimizers comes into play. Most real-world studies depend on how the researcher posits the strategic and tactical questions that clients should get asked before any data collection gets underway.

In sum, I have found Sawtooth Software to be a one-stop-shopping experience for virtually any question dealing with trade-off analysis and related techniques. Orme's book should facilitate the learning process even more. Through Sawtooth Software's conferences and internal research on best practices, conjoint analysis has both matured and flowered as a practical set of tools for designing new (or refurbished) products and services.

As for me, the excellent glossary gets my vote for the best part of the book by far. This glossary must have taken eons to write. And the meticulous results justify the immense effort that has gone into the whole enterprise.

Paul E. Green, Professor Emeritus of Marketing
University of Pennsylvania
Spring 2005

Preface

Over the years, I have heard colleagues lament that there is not a single book that provides a good overview and introduction to conjoint analysis. The conjoint books that are currently available (at least the ones I know about) tend to be academic and assume a solid background in statistics. The goal with this work is to offer a practical, accessible introduction to conjoint analysis appropriate for business managers involved in marketing and strategic planning, research analysts, and, of course, university students.

This work assembles and updates a series of introductory articles I have written over the years, previously published on my company's Web site:

http://www.sawtoothsoftware.com

Chapter 2, chapter 13, and the glossary are new with this publication. Admittedly, this work is heavily steeped in the Sawtooth Software perspective. Yet, my intention is that readers who do not use Sawtooth Software's systems will find much of general applicability and value.

One of the greatest challenges in learning about conjoint analysis is grasping and reconciling the vocabulary. Not only is the terminology extensive, but different authors refer to precisely the same thing using different words. To help the reader, appendix A features a glossary of terms. If you encounter terms you do not recognize, you may want to check the glossary for assistance.

Bryan K. Orme, Sawtooth Software
Sequim, Washington
Spring 2009

Acknowledgments

In assembling this work, I am indebted to Rich Johnson, who has served as a patient mentor to me over the last fifteen years and who has reviewed and helped edit these articles. Paul Green was immensely gracious to provide suggestions and write the foreword. It means the world to me that the "father of conjoint analysis" would do this. Paul is truly a gentleman.

The chapter on industry applications of conjoint analysis would not have been possible without the generous contributions of Greg Rogers, Mike Lotti, Liana Fraenkel, Jim Christian, Calvin Bierley, Murray Rudd, Charles Cunningham, Margaret Kruk, Peter Rockers, and Chris Chapman. Because these individuals do not work at consulting companies, they had little motivation other than the desire to contribute to the cause of championing tradeoff analysis and to help me personally. Some of these individuals had to secure the approval of their legal departments to get their stories released. Their persistence is deeply appreciated.

Many thanks also to Tom Eagle and Keith Chrzan for their review and comments on the glossary. These two are some of the finest people and most capable conjoint analysts I have known. They caught a number of mistakes. I accept responsibility for any remaining errors.

I am also grateful for my association with quality individuals who have contributed to my academic and professional development: Joel Huber, Dick Wittink, Jon Pinnell, Karlan Witt, and Peter Zandan.

And, of course, this book would not have been possible without the vision and enthusiasm of Tom Miller at Research Publishers LLC. He and his able copy-editors, Gypsy Fleischman and Kristin Gill, transformed a document with rough graphics and prose into a truly professional piece. Tom went the extra mile in developing graphics and choosing a memorable cover to make sure this book had aesthetic appeal—a talent that escapes me.

My long-term employment at Sawtooth Software has been a dream experience. Thank you, Rich, for seeing my potential and bringing me to Sawtooth Software. I treasure my relationship with my Sawtooth colleagues and our customers as well. Chris King, former president of Sawtooth Software and a close friend, deserves many thanks for encouraging this effort.

Above all, I am indebted to two key women in my life: my mother Cecelia and especially my wife Chandra. Mom instilled in me a desire for education and excellence. My wife (who is ever so more intelligent than I) loves me despite my many flaws and works tirelessly in support of me and our seven children. Thank you, dear, for your sacrifice and devotion.

Bryan K. Orme, Sawtooth Software
Sequim, Washington
Spring 2009

Figures

Tables

Exhibits

Chapter 1

Managerial Overview
of Conjoint Analysis

A great deal of market research commissioned today is descriptive in nature rather than predictive. Descriptive information is useful to characterize demographics, usage patterns, and attitudes of individuals. Beyond descriptive information, managers need survey research tools that can predict what consumers will buy when faced with the variety of brands available and myriad product characteristics. It is precisely due to this focus that conjoint or trade-off analysis has become so popular over the last three decades.

Humans employ a variety of heuristics when evaluating product alternatives and choosing in the marketplace. Many products are made up of a dizzying array of features (e.g., computers, cell phone calling programs, insurance policies, and manufacturing equipment), whereas some are more straightforward (e.g., yogurt, beverages, and light bulbs) and are mainly differentiated by brand, packaging, and price. How does the manager decide what product characteristics, packaging, and branding to use or what price to charge to maximize profits? And how does the consumer evaluate the offering vis-à-vis other alternatives in the marketplace?

To decide what product to sell, managers may use their own intuition or the recommendations of design engineers, or they may look to competitors for indications of what already works. These strategies are myopic and reactive. In consumer-oriented organizations, potential products are often evaluated through concept (market) tests. Buyers are shown a product concept and asked questions regarding their purchase interest, or new products are actually placed in test markets. These tests can be quite expensive and time consuming, and generally investigate just one or a few variations of a product concept. In some surveys, research respondents are asked to rate brands and products or to check which brands and product features they prefer. None of these approaches by itself has been consistently successful and cost-efficient. Conjoint analysis uses the best elements of these techniques in a cost-effective survey research approach.

Back in the early 1970s, marketing academics (Green and Rao 1971) applied the notion of conjoint measurement, which had been proposed by mathematical psychologists (Luce and Tukey 1964), to solve these complex problems. The general idea was that humans evaluate the overall desirability of a complex product or service based on a function of the value of its separate (yet conjoined) parts. In the simplest form, one might assume an additive model. Consider a PC purchase. A consumer browsing the Internet might see the following alternative:

> Dell
> 3 GHz processor
> 2GB RAM
> 17-inch flat panel display
> $899

Assuming that this consumer uses some internal, subconscious additive point system to evaluate the overall attractiveness of the offer, the unobserved scores (called part-worths) for the attributes of this product for a given buyer might be

Attribute	Part-worth
Dell	20
3 GHz processor	50
2 GB RAM	5
17-inch flat panel display	15
$899	30
Total utility	120

The estimated overall utility or desirability of this product alternative is equal to the sum of its parts, or 120 utiles. The trick is to obtain these scores from individuals for the variety of attributes we might include in the product or that our competitors might include. To do this reliably, one first develops a list of attributes and multiple levels or degrees within each:

Brand	Processor	RAM	Display	Price
Dell	2 GHz	1 GB	17-inch	$699
Gateway	3 GHz	2 GB	19-inch	$899
HP	4 GHz	3 GB	21-inch	$1,099
Sony				

It is easy to see that there are many possible combinations of these attribute levels. In the 1970s, it became popular to print each of many product profiles on separate cards and ask respondents to evaluate them by ranking or rating. Consider the conjoint rating question in exhibit 1.1.

By systematically varying the features of the product and observing how respondents react to the resulting product profiles, one can statistically deduce (typically using linear regression) the scores (part-worths) for the separate features re-

How likely are you to purchase this computer?
Use a scale from 0 to 100, where 1 = *not at all likely*,
and 100 = *definitely would purchase.*

HP
3 GHz processor
1 GB RAM
17-inch display
$1,099

Exhibit 1.1. Conjoint rating question

spondents may have been subconsciously using to evaluate products. In contrast to answering direct questions about individual product features, conjoint survey respondents cannot simply say that all features are important—they must trade off different aspects of the product (as in real life), weighing alternatives that have both highly desirable and less desirable qualities.

Using the attribute list developed earlier, there are $(4 \times 3 \times 3 \times 3 \times 3)$ or 324 possible product profiles that could be considered. But what makes conjoint analysis work so nicely is that an individual respondent does not have to evaluate all possible product profiles. If we are willing to assume a simple additive model (which tends to work well in practice), each respondent needs to evaluate only a fraction of the total combinations. With our example, only about eighteen to twenty-four carefully chosen product concepts (using experimental design principles of independence and balance) would need to be evaluated to lead to a complete set of part-worth scores for each respondent for all sixteen attribute levels. The part-worth scores are useful for determining which levels are preferred, and the relative importance of each attribute. Once we know these scores, we can simply sum them to predict how each respondent would react to any of the 324 possible product profiles.

Although the scores on the attribute levels provide significant value in and of themselves, the real value of conjoint analysis comes from the what-if market simulators that can easily be developed, often within spreadsheets. It follows that if, for each respondent, we can predict the overall desirability for all possible product profile combinations (given the set of attribute levels we measured), we can also predict how each respondent might choose if faced with a choice among two or more competing profiles. For example, we can simulate what percent of the market would prefer each of four PCs (described using the different brands and performance characteristics we measured) if available for purchase. These predictions across a sample of respondents are referred to as shares of choice or shares of preference.

Holding competitive offerings constant, managers can systematically vary the features of their own product profile (such as pricing or performance attributes) and observe what percent of the market would prefer their product under each condition. With conjoint simulators, managers can estimate demand curves and substitution effects, answering questions like, "From which competitors do we take the most share if we increase the processor speed?" They can assess cannibalization effects: "What happens to our overall share if we come out with another product with lesser performance at a lower price?" In essence, managers have the ability to estimate the results of millions of possible concept/market tests based on data collected in a single survey research project among, typically, 300 to 600 respondents. If additional information is included, such as feature costs, computer search algorithms can find optimal product configurations (holding a set of competitors constant) to maximize share, revenue, or profit.

Since the 1970s, as one might expect, additional improvements and refinements have been made to conjoint analysis. In the 1980s, a computerized version of conjoint analysis called Adaptive Conjoint Analysis (ACA) was developed, which could customize the conjoint interview for each respondent, focusing on the attributes, levels, and trade-offs that were most relevant to each respondent (Johnson 1987b). As a result, more attributes and levels could be studied effectively. In the 1990s, it became popular to ask respondents to simply choose among product profiles rather than rate each profile individually on a numeric scale. The feeling was that buyers in the real world do not actually score each alternative on a rating scale prior to choosing—they simply choose. With choice-based conjoint (CBC), respondents answer perhaps twelve to twenty-four choice questions such as the one in exhibit 1.2.

Although each question takes longer to read (because there are multiple alternatives to consider), choice-based conjoint questions seem more realistic and can include a *none* choice that can be selected if none of the products would appeal to the survey respondent. New developments in computationally intensive statistical methods (hierarchical Bayes estimation) make it possible to estimate a complete set of part-worth scores on each attribute level for each respondent (Allenby, Arora, and Ginter 1995). The results are typically better than with ratings-based conjoint, and the resulting "what-if" market simulators are usually more accurate in predicting actual market choices.

Today, thousands of conjoint studies are conducted each year over the Internet, via hand-held and mobile technologies, by fax, using person-to-person interviews, or by mailed paper surveys. Leading organizations are saving a great deal of money on research and development costs, successfully using the results to design new products or line extensions, to reposition existing products, and to make more profitable pricing decisions.

If you were in the market to purchase a PC today,
and if these were your only alternatives,
which would you choose?

Dell	HP	Sony	None:
4 GHz processor	3 GHz processor	2 GHz processor	If these were
3 GB RAM	2 GB RAM	1 GB RAM	my only choices,
21-inch display	19-inch display	17-inch display	I'd defer my
$1,099	$899	$699	purchase.
⚫	⚫	⚫	⚫

Exhibit 1.2. Choice-based conjoint question

Chapter 2

How Conjoint Analysis Works

Conjoint or trade-off analysis has become one of today's most commonly used market research tools for designing and pricing products and services. This chapter is designed to give newcomers to this exciting field some insight into how conjoint analysis works.

You will fill out a simple conjoint or trade-off survey dealing with different credit card offers. Please have a hand calculator available, so you can analyze the results of your survey. The calculations will be simple, involving only addition, division, and taking the average of three values at a time. I hope that by the end of this exercise I will have demystified conjoint analysis and you will have gained some insight into how this popular research method works.

2.1 Marketing Problem and Attribute List

Imagine that a credit card company is interested in how consumers trade off various aspects of credit card offerings, specifically, the brand, interest rate, and credit limit. A market researcher might approach the problem with conjoint analysis. First, a list of attributes and levels is developed that captures the range of brands, interest rates, and credit limits under consideration:

Brand	Interest Rate	Credit Limit
Visa	10%	$2,500
MasterCard	15%	$5,000
Discover	20%	$7,500

With three attributes each at three levels, there are $(3 \times 3 \times 3) = 27$ possible credit card combinations. In the 1970s, researchers often printed each product profile in the conjoint survey on cards. Exhibit 2.1 is an illustration of one of the twenty-seven credit card combinations.

7

How much do you like this credit card offer?
Use a scale from 0 to 10, where 0 = not at all
and 10 = very much. Write your answer
in the blank box.

Discover
20% interest
$5,000 credit limit

Exhibit 2.1. A conjoint card

With conjoint analysis, we rarely ask respondents to evaluate all possible combinations of attributes because this would create impossibly long questionnaires in most cases. Instead, we use abbreviated study plans that focus upon subsets of all possible combinations of attributes. Abbreviated study plans may be found in reference books of experimental designs, or they may be generated by specialized computer programs.

2.2 Survey Design Plan

This chapter illustrates the simplest form of conjoint analysis: traditional full-profile conjoint. This is the original conjoint method (Green and Rao 1971). We show various credit card possibilities, referred to (coincidentally) as cards. The selected combinations of attributes or product profiles are called the design plan. Exhibit 2.2 shows the design plan for the conjoint analysis survey you are about to complete. Each row represents a conjoint analysis question or card. There are nine questions in the survey, with attribute combinations shown by the X marks in the exhibit. Exhibit 2.1 shows the first card of this survey: Discover, 20% interest, $5,000 credit limit.

This design plan has some valuable properties. First, you may notice that each level is shown exactly three times. Therefore, the plan is balanced. A clever aspect of this plan is that each level appears exactly once with every other level from the other attributes. For example, Visa appears once at each of the levels of interest rate and credit limit. A similar relationship holds for the other two brands and for any combination of attributes taken two at a time. This property makes it possible to estimate the independent effect of each attribute with a relatively high

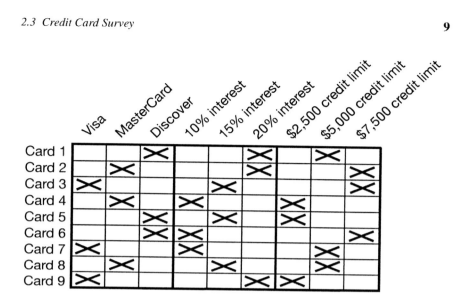

Exhibit 2.2. Credit card design plan

degree of precision. For example, it would be difficult to distinguish the separate effects of brand and interest rate if Visa always appeared with the lowest interest rate. Would the preference for such a concept be due to the desirability of Visa or the low interest rate?

2.3 Credit Card Survey

Now that I have given an introduction to conjoint analysis and design plans, please complete a survey as if you were choosing a new credit card. Drawing upon the design plan, exhibit 2.3 presents nine credit card offers to be evaluated. For each credit card offer, you are asked, "How much do you like this credit card offer?" Use a ten-point scale to score each offer, where 0 means "not at all" and 10 means "very much." After you have completed the credit card survey, rank the credit card offers in the final exercise (exhibit 2.5 on page 17).

I hope you found the credit card survey interesting. You probably also found it a bit challenging. To evaluate the cards, you probably developed a strategy. Perhaps you decided early on which attribute was most important to you, and you based your decision on that aspect. Perhaps each of the attributes carried about equal weight in your decision, and you needed to decide how much of one you were willing to give up for the other. You probably did not find an offer that was exactly what you wanted in every way. So it is with real purchase decisions. Consumers make these kinds of trade-offs every day.

*Show how much you like each of the nine credit card offers
below by writing your answers in the blank boxes.
Use a scale from 0 to 10, where 0 = not at all and 10 = very much.*

1 Discover 20% interest $5,000 credit limit	2 MasterCard 20% interest $7,500 credit limit	3 Visa 15% interest $7,500 credit limit
4 MasterCard 10% interest $2,500 credit limit	5 Discover 15% interest $2,500 credit limit	6 Discover 10% interest $7,500 credit limit
7 Visa 10% interest $5,000 credit limit	8 MasterCard 15% interest $5,000 credit limit	9 Visa 20% interest $2,500 credit limit

Exhibit 2.3. Credit card survey

Now you are about to learn why conjoint analysis is so useful to managers and market research analysts. Based on the credit card ratings you provided, you will compute a weight or part-worth utility for each of the attribute levels. The set of weights would account for your overall credit card ratings. After all, you probably were loosely applying some sort of unconscious scoring mechanism or system of preference weights. Conjoint analysis seeks to uncover that system of preference weights. Human decision making is undoubtedly complex, and a simple set of weights can never fully capture the complexities. Conjoint analysis tends to do a very good job despite the model simplifications.

2.4 Conjoint Analysis Utilities

Because each attribute level appeared exactly once with every other level in the study, there is a simple way to estimate attribute level utilities (also known as part-worths). Of course, conjoint studies in the real world are rarely so straightforward. I have constructed this example so that the utility estimation may be done with a hand calculator. For this simple illustration, the utility estimate for each level is the average score for cards that include that level. Instructions for the calculations are provided in exhibit 2.4. Please compute the utility scores for each level now. If all has gone well, the utility scores should make intuitive sense to you. The higher the score for a level, the more desirable that level. It often helps to visualize data or to plot utility scores on a line chart. Please plot your part-worth utility values for each attribute in figure 2.1, drawing lines connecting the points on each graph.

2.5 Importance Scores

Some researchers calculate an importance score for each attribute. An importance score reflects the effect each attribute has upon product choice, given the range of levels we included in the questionnaire. The calculations are straightforward, and you will again be able to use a hand calculator. Use figure 2.2 to work on your calculations. Refer to chapter 8 (page 80) or the glossary (page 171) for examples of importance score calculations. After you have finished calculating importance scores, you can plot them on the bar chart in figure 2.3.

2.6 Conjoint Analysis as a Predictive Model of Choice

Charts of utilities and importance scores are useful, but a what-if market simulator that can be built using conjoint results is the most valuable tool for managers. A market simulator uses the utility scores to predict which product alternatives respondents would choose within competitive scenarios. The predictions can be made not only for the few product alternatives that were actually shown to respondents, but also for the often thousands or more potential combinations that were not shown.

Record your survey responses in the blank boxes for the numbered cards. The rating for each credit card offer is recorded in three groupings: once for the brand, for the interest rate, and for the credit limit.

Then compute the average rating across the three cards in each row.

Attribute Level	Survey Responses (0-to-10 rating scale)			Row Average (Utiilty Score)
Visa	Card 3 ☐	Card 7 ☐	Card 9 ☐	
MasterCard	Card 2 ☐	Card 4 ☐	Card 8 ☐	
Discover	Card 1 ☐	Card 5 ☐	Card 6 ☐	
10% interest	Card 4 ☐	Card 6 ☐	Card 7 ☐	
15% interest	Card 3 ☐	Card 5 ☐	Card 8 ☐	
20% interest	Card 1 ☐	Card 2 ☐	Card 9 ☐	
$2,500 credit limit	Card 4 ☐	Card 5 ☐	Card 9 ☐	
$5,000 credit limit	Card 1 ☐	Card 7 ☐	Card 8 ☐	
$7,500 credit limit	Card 2 ☐	Card 3 ☐	Card 6 ☐	

Exhibit 2.4. Estimating part-worth utilities from a conjoint survey

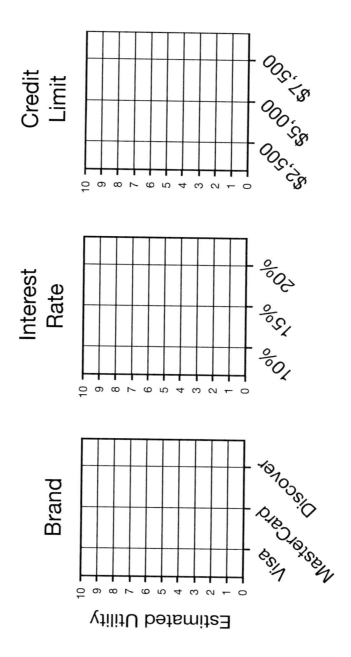

Figure 2.1. Line chart of part-worth utilities for attribute levels

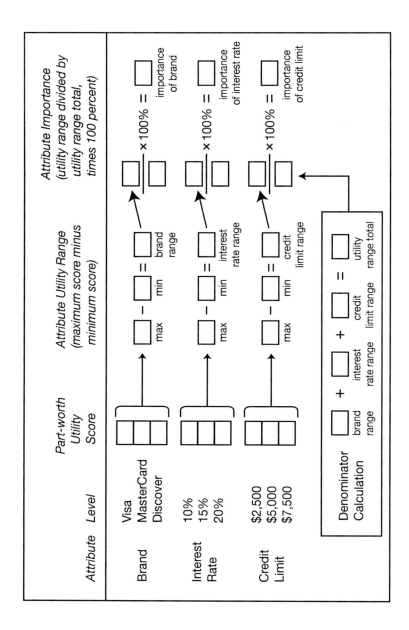

Figure 2.2. Calculating importance scores

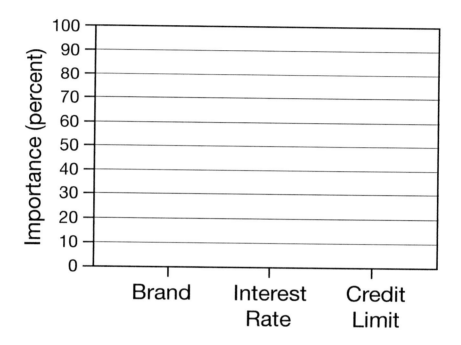

Figure 2.3. Bar chart of importance scores

In the example you have completed, there were only twenty-seven possible credit card configurations. You evaluated nine of them, from which you estimated part-worth utilities. But you also rank-ordered the three additional credit card offers in exhibit 2.5. These were holdout cards, credit card offers that were not used in developing your utility values. How well do your conjoint utility values predict how you ranked these three additional alternatives?

Add utility values that correspond to the attribute levels on each credit card to determine the total utility of that card (you need to add three part-worth values for each card). Compare the predicted total utilities to the rankings you previously provided in exhibit 2.5. If you completed the exercise carefully, the predictions should closely resemble your actual choices.

I hope this exercise has been useful and that you now understand how conjoint analysis works. If you answered the original and holdout questions carefully, it may surprise you how accurate the results from such a simple exercise can be. Of course, conjoint analysis in practice is more involved than what I have demonstrated here. Design plans are rarely as simple as portrayed here, and there are more powerful and accurate estimation techniques than taking simple averages. Chapter 8 expands upon these ideas, providing a brief introduction to estimating conjoint utilities using multiple regression. For more information about how to interpret your utilities and importance scores, see chapter 9 entitled "Interpreting the Results of Conjoint Analysis."

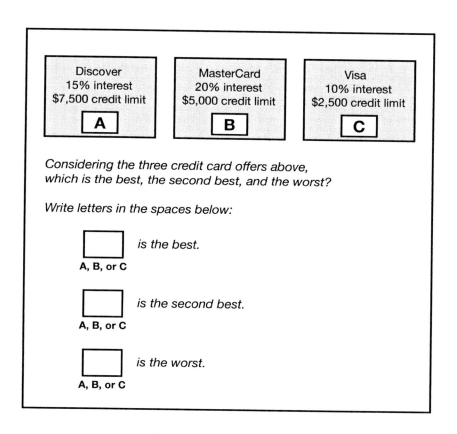

Exhibit 2.5. Final exercise

Chapter 3

Understanding the Value of Conjoint Analysis

Market researchers face two main challenges as they provide market intelligence for managers: to meet managers' objectives with useful, valid results and to communicate those results effectively. Failure on either of these points is fatal. Conjoint analysis provides useful results that, when presented well, are easy for managers to embrace and understand. It is no wonder that conjoint analysis is the most rapidly growing and one of the most widely used market research techniques today. This chapter discusses the benefits of conjoint analysis and finishes by highlighting a dangerous pitfall to avoid when presenting market simulators.

3.1 Realism Begets Better Data

Even though conjoint analysis involves more sophisticated survey design and analysis, and more effort by respondents, simpler approaches can be unrealistic, even useless. Suppose we were conducting a study about laptop computers, and using a survey like the one in exhibit 3.1. Respondents can answer importance survey questions quickly. A recent research project recorded an average time per response of five seconds (Orme 2003). Most respondents answer with high ratings, while the bottom half of the scale is largely ignored. This results in sub-par data for statistical analysis: skewed distributions, with typically little differentiation between attributes. Such self-explicated importances reveal little about how to build a better laptop. How much battery life will buyers trade off for a given increase in processor speed? Further, stated importances often do not reflect true values. It may be socially desirable to say price is unimportant—after all, respondents do not want to appear cheap. Yet in real-world laptop purchases, price may become a critical factor.

This chapter is adapted from an article published in *Quirk's Market Research Review*, March 1996.

When purchasing a laptop computer, how important is . . .

(Circle one number per item)

	Not Important								Very Important
Brand	1	2	3	4	5	6	7	8	9
Battery life	1	2	3	4	5	6	7	8	9
Processor speed	1	2	3	4	5	6	7	8	9
Weight	1	2	3	4	5	6	7	8	9
Price	1	2	3	4	5	6	7	8	9

Exhibit 3.1. Importance survey questions

Even though it is much easier on respondents to ask them to complete a grid such as shown in exhibit 3.1, these importance questions are not very meaningful. Buyers cannot always get the best of everything in the real world. They must make difficult trade-offs and concessions. When survey respondents (just like buyers) are forced to make difficult trade-offs, we learn the true value of product alternatives. And rather than ask respondents to react to generic terms like "battery life," we ask them to react to specific, realistic product specifications. The results are both meaningful and managerially actionable.

Conjoint analysis aims for greater realism, grounds attributes in concrete descriptions, and results in better discrimination among attribute importances. Conjoint analysis creates a more appropriate context for research. Consider a pairwise trade-off question featuring laptop computers. See exhibit 3.2.

Of course, conjoint questions can also be asked one product profile at a time, as in a traditional card sort. The rationale behind pairwise comparisons is this: People can make finer distinctions when they directly compare objects. For example, if someone hands you a four-pound rock, takes it away, and then hands you a five-pound rock, chances are you will not be able to tell which is heavier. But if you hold one rock in each hand, you will have a much better chance of guessing which weighs more. Despite the probable benefits of pairwise comparisons, we conducted a research study and found virtually no difference in the results for one-profile versus pairwise traditional conjoint analysis (Orme and King 1998).

Another flavor of conjoint analysis offers even greater realism and extends the idea of side-by-side comparisons: choice-based conjoint (Louviere and Woodworth 1983; Sawtooth Software 1993). For a choice-based conjoint question about laptop computers, see exhibit 3.3.

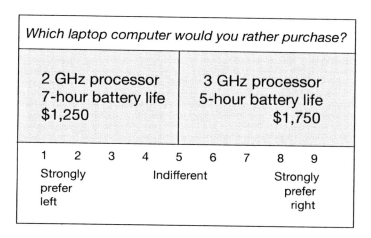

Exhibit 3.2. Pairwise trade-off question

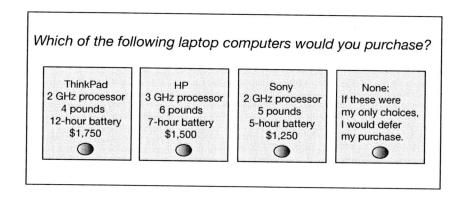

Exhibit 3.3. Choice-based conjoint question

Choice-based conjoint questions closely mimic what buyers do in the real world—choose among available offerings. Including *none* as an option enhances the realism, and allows those respondents who are not likely to purchase to express their disinterest. Choice-based data reflect choices, not just preferences. If we agree that the ultimate goal of market simulators is to predict choice, then it is only natural that we would value choice-based data.

Some managers do not have the training in statistics to grasp the concept of orthogonal designs, main effects assumptions, or part-worth utility estimation. More technical folks, utilizing specialized software, can manage these details. Whether statisticians or otherwise, almost everyone can grasp the idea that realistic models result from realistic questioning methods, and they can be comforted that conjoint analysis is a reliable, time-proven method.

3.2 Brand Equity

Conjoint analysis provides useful results for product development, pricing research, competitive positioning, and market segmentation. It can also measure brand equity, which is an especially critical issue for many managers.

Brand equity encompasses the intangible forces in the market that allow a product with a brand name to be worth more to buyers than one without. High-equity brands command higher prices and are less price elastic. Because brand equity goes directly to the bottom line, it is no surprise that managers are focused on it.

Choice-based conjoint offers a reliable way to measure brand equity. Choice-based conjoint presents respondents with varying product configurations and asks which they would purchase or choose. Each brand is presented at various prices throughout the interview. The percentage of times respondents choose each brand at each price point reveals preference and price sensitivity for the brands. Compelling demand curves result when we plot the probability of choice by price and connect the points with smooth lines. See figure 3.1 for hypothetical demand curves for three brands of pain reliever: Renew, Balmex, and PainFree.

If the brand manager for Renew wants to quantify the price premium it commands over the other brands, choice-based conjoint analysis reveals the answer. We can use the demand curves from figure 3.1 as a starting point: We draw a horizontal line through points A, B, and C representing a level of equal relative demand or preference. If Renew is priced at $3.90 and Balmex at $3.50, respondents on average will be indifferent (have the same preference) between the two. This forty-cent difference (point C price minus point B price or $3.90 minus $3.50) represents the premium or brand equity that Renew commands over Balmex. Similarly, Renew commands a sixty-cent premium over PainFree (point C price minus point A price). See figure 3.2.

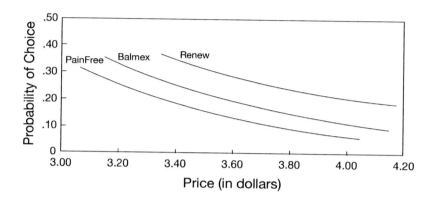

Figure 3.1. Choice-based conjoint demand curves

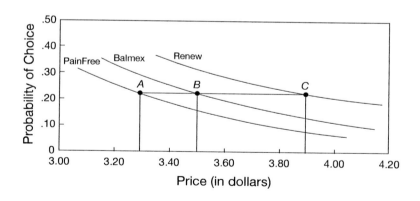

Figure 3.2. Estimating brand equity using points of equal relative demand

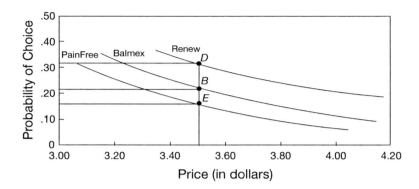

Figure 3.3. Estimating brand equity using points of equal price

Another approach to assessing brand equity results from comparing preferences with all brands offered at the same price. Imagine that we continue drawing the vertical line from $3.50 through point B until it intersects Renew's demand curve. That point represents a relative preference or choice probability of 0.32. At $3.50, Balmex and PainFree have choice probabilities of 0.22 and 0.16, respectively. See figure 3.3 with labeled points D, B, and E for Renew, Balmex, and PainFree, respectively, at the selected price point of $3.50. Brand equity may be estimated by using ratios of choice probabilities or percentages. At the selected price point of $3.50, Renew is preferred to Balmex by a ratio of $\frac{32}{22}$, or it has 45 percent higher preference than Balmex. Similarly, Renew is preferred to PainFree by a ratio of $\frac{32}{16}$ or 100 percent over PainFree.

3.3 Strategic Pricing Research

In an ideal world, researchers could accurately measure price sensitivity by manipulating prices in test markets and measuring changes in demand. While scanner technology has made this sort of analysis more feasible than ever before for many categories of consumer goods, these real-world experiments often face significant hurdles. Markets do not remain constant for the duration of the experiment. Macroeconomic forces can alter demand. Competitors can change their prices and/or promotions. Buyers can stock up to take advantage of lower prices. And new products may be introduced. While conjoint pricing experiments are not as realistic as the real-world event, conjoint experiments hold market forces constant. They can test price ranges or new products outside of current offerings.

In the demand curve example, Renew holds the enviable position of being preferred to Balmex and PainFree at all price levels. Notice also that the demand curves in exhibits 3.1 through 3.3 are not parallel. Renew's preference declines at a slower rate than the other brands' as price increases. Respondents are less price sensitive toward Renew than the other brands. The ability to more directly measure unique price sensitivities by brand is an advantage choice-based conjoint enjoys over traditional main-effects-only conjoint analysis. While it is true that differential price sensitivities can be observed through sensitivity simulations from traditional full-profile conjoint analysis, most researchers believe that choice-based conjoint captures more accurate information about price sensitivity.

Demand curves provide strategic information for pricing decisions. Suppose Renew is the market leader. Renew's manager is considering initiating a price cut, and her past experience suggests that the discount brands will react with similar price cuts. She could learn a great deal using conjoint data—enough to avoid a mistake. The slopes of the demand curves show that, if prices were lowered, Renew would gain share at a slower rate than Balmex or PainFree. So if she lowers the price and the other brands follow, Renew's market share and profits would decrease.

Price elasticity can be quantified for each brand by examining the ratio of preference at the highest price versus preference at the lowest price. Alternatively, the price elasticity of demand (defined as percentage change in quantity demanded divided by percentage change in price) can be easily calculated for each brand in a choice-based conjoint study.

Some managers have been so pleased with this approach to strategic pricing research that they have funded wave after wave of conjoint tracking studies. They compare demand curves across time periods to quantify changes in brand equity, to gauge the results of previous pricing or other marketing mix changes, and to formulate future strategy.

Choice-based conjoint analysis has proven very useful and generally accurate for pricing decisions, especially when it comes to fast moving consumer goods. As an example, price sensitivity measurements by conjoint analysis for various Procter & Gamble products were shown to match well (on average) the price sensitivities calculated from econometric models applied to actual sales data (Renkin, Rogers, and Huber 2004).

3.4 Preference, Not Market Share

About fifteen years ago, We were involved in a choice-based conjoint study for a manufacturer of personal computers. Our main contact was the pricing manager whose objectives were to measure market awareness, preference, and price sensitivity for his sub-brands and major competitors. We conducted the study disk-by-mail and were soon delivering top-line conjoint results. This was prior to data collection over the Internet, so respondents received their computerized interviews on 3.5-inch floppy disks.

Our client was skeptical when he saw that the conjoint analysis reported that one of the company's newly released brands, call it FastPC, was preferred to its well-established brands. The client insisted that this could not be right and that we check the data. We did—somewhat nervously, we might add—but found no errors. In the meantime, he called his sales department for a sanity check. Sales reported that FastPC was flying off the shelf. FastPC had exceeded all expectations.

While this happy-ending story warms us inside, it also illustrates a limitation of conjoint analysis. Conjoint analysis predicts preference, not market share. While the newly released FastPC was selling above expectations, its market share at that point fell short of established brands. Given enough time, adequate promotion, and distribution, we would expect FastPC's market share to align more closely with conjoint results.

Conjoint models do not predict market share due to a variety of reasons, including the following:

- Conjoint analysis assumes perfect information. In the conjoint interview, respondents are educated about available brands and features. In the real world, obscure brands have less chance of being purchased. Conjoint analysis cannot fully account for differences in awareness developed through advertising and promotion.
- Conjoint analysis assumes that all products are equally available. One brand is as conveniently selected as another in a conjoint interview.
- Respondents might not accurately reflect potential buyers. Many will not have the interest, authority, or ability to purchase.
- Results from conjoint analysis reflect the potential market acceptance of products and services, given proper promotion, distribution, and time.

Many researchers quantify factors that conjoint analysis cannot account for and build them back into the model using external effect adjustments. While this practice typically brings conjoint results more closely in line with actual market share, it draws us into a troublesome paradox. As more factors are accounted for and as we more accurately tune the conjoint model to market share, we start to believe that we have actually developed a valid market share predictor.

Believing that we have an accurate predictor of market share can lead us to misuse a model. That said, conjoint models are excellent directional indicators. Conjoint analysis can reveal product modifications that can increase market share, but it will probably not reveal how much actual market share will increase. Conjoint analysis can tell us that the market is more price sensitive for Brand A than Brand B, but we probably do not know the exact price sensitivity of either one. Conjoint analysis can identify which market segment will be most likely to purchase your client's product, but probably not the exact number of units that will be purchased.

The market simulator is usually the most anticipated deliverable for managers. Do not let this enthusiasm get out of hand. Conjoint simulators are directional indicators that can provide a great deal of information about relative feature importances and preferences for product configurations. While conjoint simulators are excellent tools for revealing strategic moves that can improve the success of a product, they are not infallible market share predictors. Many other factors, such as awareness, distribution, advertising, and product life cycles, drive market share in the real world. Conjoint models can be fine-tuned to account partially for these elements, but we must avoid thinking that adjusted conjoint models can consistently and accurately predict volumetric absolutes such as market share. The only exception to this rule follows from careful validation based on real sales data, establishing a clear link between the calibrated conjoint model and sales volume for the specific product category and market in question.

Conjoint analysis increases the return on research dollars by providing managers with useful, valid information. Its realism leads to more accurate results and provides a strategic tool for quantifying brand equity and relative price sensitivity. To ensure success, researchers must carefully set management expectations regarding what conjoint analysis can and cannot do.

Chapter 4

A Short History of Conjoint Analysis

The genesis of new statistical models has rarely been within the field of marketing research. Marketing researchers have mainly borrowed from other fields. Conjoint analysis and the more recent discrete choice or choice-based conjoint methods are no exception. Conjoint methods were based on work in the sixties by mathematical psychologists and statisticians Luce and Tukey (1964), and discrete choice methods came from econometrics, building upon the work of McFadden (1974), 2000 Nobel Prize winner in economics.

Marketers sometimes have thought (or been taught) that the word "conjoint" refers to respondents evaluating features of products or services "CONsidered JOINTly." In reality, the adjective "conjoint" derives from the verb "to conjoin," meaning "joined together." The key characteristic of conjoint analysis is that respondents evaluate product profiles composed of multiple conjoined elements (attributes or features). Based on how respondents evaluate the combined elements (the product concepts), we deduce the preference scores that they might have assigned to individual components of the product that would have resulted in those overall evaluations. Essentially, it is a back-door, decompositional approach to estimating people's preferences for features rather than an explicit, compositional approach of simply asking respondents to rate the various features. The fundamental premise is that people cannot reliably express how they weight separate features of the product, but we can tease these out using the more realistic approach of asking for evaluations of product concepts through conjoint analysis.

Let us not deceive ourselves. Human decision making and the formation of preferences is complex, capricious, and ephemeral. Traditional conjoint analysis makes some heroic assumptions, including the proposition that the value of a product is equal to the sum of the values of its parts (i.e., simple additivity), and that complex decision making can be explained using a limited number of dimensions. Despite the leaps of faith, conjoint analysis tends to work well in practice, and gives managers, engineers, and marketers the insight they need to reduce un-

---

This chapter is based upon an article first published in *Quirk's Market Research Review*, July/August 2004.

```
Made in Europe
Rear-wheel drive
Four-door
$18,000
```

Exhibit 4.1. Conjoint card for automobiles

certainty when facing important decisions. Conjoint analysis is not perfect, but we do not need it to be. With all its assumptions and imperfections, it still trumps other methods.

4.1   Early Conjoint Analysis (1960s and 1970s)

Just prior to 1970, marketing professor Paul Green recognized that Luce and Tukey's (1964) article on conjoint measurement, published in a non-marketing journal, might be applied to marketing problems: to understand how buyers made complex purchase decisions, to estimate preferences and importances for product features, and to predict buyer behavior. Green could not have envisioned the profound impact his work on full-profile card-sort conjoint analysis would eventually achieve when he and coauthor Rao published their historic article "Conjoint Measurement for Quantifying Judgmental Data" in the *Journal of Marketing Research (JMR)* (Green and Rao 1971).

With early full-profile conjoint analysis, researchers carefully constructed a deck of conjoint cards based on published catalogs of orthogonal design plans. Each card described a product profile, such as shown in exhibit 4.1 for automobiles.

Respondents evaluated each of perhaps eighteen separate cards and sorted them in order from best to worst. Based on the observed orderings, researchers could statistically deduce, for each individual, which attributes were most important and which levels were most preferred. The card-sort approach seemed to work quite well as long as the number of attributes studied did not become too large. And researchers soon found that better data could be obtained by asking respondents to rate each card (say, on a ten-point scale of desirability) and using

	Made in USA	Made in Europe	Made in Far East
Front-wheel drive	7	6	3
Rear-wheel drive	9	8	5
All-wheel drive	4	2	1

Exhibit 4.2. Johnson's trade-off matrix with rank-order data

ordinary least squares regression analysis to derive the respondent preferences. In 1975 Green and Wind published an article in *Harvard Business Review* on measuring consumer judgments for carpet cleaners, and business leaders soon took notice of this new method.

Also just prior to 1970, a practitioner named Richard Johnson at Market Facts was working independently to solve a difficult client problem involving a durable goods product and trade-offs among twenty-eight separate product features, each having about five different realizations or levels. The problem was much more complex than those being solved by Green and coauthors with full-profile card-sort conjoint analysis, and Johnson invented a clever method of pairwise trade-offs. His paper on trade-off matrices was published in *JMR* (Johnson 1974). Rather than asking respondents to evaluate all attributes at the same time in full profile, Johnson broke the problem down into focused trade-offs involving just two attributes at a time. Respondents were asked to rank-order the cells within each table in terms of preference for the conjoined levels.

In exhibit 4.2 we see a respondent who liked the all-wheel drive vehicle made in the Far East best and the rear-wheel drive vehicle made in the United States least. With Johnson's trade-off matrices, respondents would complete a number of these pairwise tables, covering all attributes in the study (but not all possible combinations of attributes). By observing the rank-ordered judgments across trade-off matrices, Johnson was able to estimate a set of preference scores and attribute importances across the entire list of attributes for each individual. Because the method only asked about two attributes at a time, a larger number of attributes could be studied than was generally thought prudent with full-profile conjoint methods.

Near the end of the 1970s, academics Paul Green and Seenu Srinivasan published an influential paper in the *Journal of Consumer Research* summarizing the use of conjoint analysis in industry, outlining new developments, and giving advice regarding best practices (Green and Srinivasan 1978).

4.2   Conjoint Analysis in the 1980s

By the early 1980s, conjoint analysis was gaining in popularity, at least among leading researchers and academics possessing considerable statistical knowledge and computer programming skills. When commercial software became available in 1985, the floodgates were opened. Based on Green's work with full-profile conjoint analysis, Steve Herman and Bretton-Clark Software released a software system for IBM personal computers.

Also in 1985, Johnson and his new company, Sawtooth Software, released a software system (also for the IBM personal computer) called Adaptive Conjoint Analysis (ACA). Over many years of working with trade-off matrices, Johnson had discovered that respondents had difficulty dealing with the numerous tables and in providing realistic answers. He discovered that he could program a computer to administer the survey and collect the data. The computer could adapt the survey to each individual in real time, asking only the most relevant trade-offs in an abbreviated, more user-friendly way that encouraged more realistic responses. Respondents seemed to enjoy taking computer surveys, and some even commented that taking an ACA survey was like playing a game of chess with the computer.

One of the most exciting aspects of these commercial conjoint analysis programs for traditional full-profile conjoint and ACA was the inclusion of what-if market simulators. Once the preferences of typically hundreds of respondents for an array of product features and levels had been captured, researchers or business managers could test the market acceptance of competitive products in a simulated competitive environment. One simply scored the various product offerings for each individual by summing the preference scores associated with each product alternative. Respondents were projected to choose the alternative with the highest preference score. The results reflected the percent of respondents in the sample that preferred each product alternative, which was called share of preference. Managers could make any number of slight modifications to their products and immediately test the likely market response by pressing a button. Under the proper conditions, these shares of preference were fairly predictive of actual market shares. The market simulator took esoteric preference scores (part-worth utilities) and converted them into something much more meaningful and actionable for managers (product shares).

Conjoint analysis quickly became the most broadly used and powerful survey-based technique for measuring and predicting consumer preference. Helping to fuel this interest was an influential case study published by Green and Wind (1989) regarding a successful application of conjoint analysis to help Marriott design its new Courtyard hotels. But the mainstreaming of conjoint analysis was not without its critics, who argued that making conjoint analysis available to the masses through user-friendly software was akin to "giving dynamite to babies."

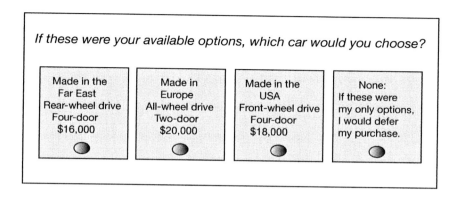

Exhibit 4.3. A choice set for automobiles

Those who experienced conjoint analysis in the late 1980s are familiar with the often acrimonious debates that ensued between two polarized camps: those advocating full-profile conjoint analysis and those in favor of ACA. In hindsight, the controversy had both positive and negative consequences. It certainly inspired research into the merits of various approaches. But it also dampened some of the enthusiasm and probably slowed the application of the technique. Some researchers and business managers paused to assess the fallout.

Prior to the release of the first two commercial conjoint analysis systems, Jordan Louviere and colleagues were adapting the idea of choice analysis among available alternatives and multinomial logit to, among other things, transportation and marketing problems. The groundwork for modeling choice among multiple alternatives had been laid by McFadden in the early 1970s. The concept of choice analysis was attractive: buyers did not rank or rate a series of products prior to purchase, they simply observed a set of available alternatives (again described in terms of conjoined features) and made a choice. From a theoretical and statistical standpoint, choice analysis was more defensible than ratings-based conjoint. But, from a practical standpoint, there were some challenges. A representative discrete choice question involving automobiles is shown in exhibit 4.3.

Discrete choice analysis seemed more realistic and natural for respondents. It offered powerful benefits, including the ability to do a better job of modeling interactions (i.e., brand-specific demand curves), availability effects, and cross-elasticities. Discrete choice analysis also had the flexibility to incorporate alternative-specific attributes and multiple constant alternatives. But the benefits came at considerable cost: discrete choice questions were an inefficient way to ask respondents questions. Respondents needed to read quite a bit of information before making a choice, and a choice only indicated which alternative was preferred rather than strength of preference.

With discrete choice there typically was not enough information to model each respondent's preferences. Rather, aggregate or summary models of preference were developed across groups of respondents. Aggregate models were subject to various problems such as independence from irrelevant alternatives (IIA or the red bus/blue bus problem) and ignorance of the separate preference functions for latent subgroups. Overcoming the problems of aggregation required building ever-more-complex models to account for attribute availability and cross-effects. These models, called mother logit models, were used by a relatively small and elite group of conjoint specialists throughout the 1980s. Given the lack of easy-to-use commercial software for fitting discrete choice models, most marketing researchers had neither the tools nor the stomach for building them.

4.3   Conjoint Analysis in the 1990s

Whereas the 1980s were characterized by a polarization of conjoint analysts into ideological camps, researchers in the 1990s came to recognize that no one conjoint method was the best approach for every problem, and expanded their repertoires. Sawtooth Software facilitated the discussion by publishing research from its users and hosting the Sawtooth Software Conference. User case studies demonstrated under what conditions various conjoint methods performed best. Sawtooth Software promoted the use of various conjoint methods by developing additional commercial software systems for full-profile conjoint analysis and discrete choice.

Based on industry usage studies conducted by leading academics (Vriens, Huber, and Wittink 1997), ACA was the most widely used conjoint technique and software system worldwide. By the end of the decade, ACA would yield that position to discrete choice analysis. Two main factors were responsible for discrete choice analysis overtaking ACA and other ratings-based conjoint methods by the turn of the century: (1) the release of commercial software for discrete choice modeling (CBC for choice-based conjoint) by Sawtooth Software in 1993 and (2) the application of hierarchical Bayes (HB) methods to estimate individual-level models from discrete choice data (principally due to articles and tutorials led by Greg Allenby of Ohio State University).

Discrete choice experiments are typically more difficult to design and analyze than traditional full-profile conjoint or ACA. Commercial software made it much easier to design and conduct CBC studies, while easy-to-use HB software made the analysis of choice data seem nearly as straightforward and familiar as the analysis of ratings-based conjoint. With individual-level models under HB, IIA and other problems due to aggregation were controlled or solved. This has helped immensely with CBC studies, especially for those designed to investigate the incremental value of line extensions or me-too imitation products. While HB transformed the way discrete choice studies were analyzed, it also provided incremental benefits for traditional ratings-based conjoint methods. Traditional conjoint methods had always estimated part-worth utilities at the individual level, but HB offered the prospect of more accurate estimation.

Other important developments during the 1990s included the following:

- Latent class models for segmenting respondents into relatively homogeneous groups, based on preferences
- Web-based data collection for all main flavors of conjoint and choice analysis
- Improvements in computer technology for presenting graphics
- Dramatic increases in computing speed and memory, making techniques such as HB feasible for common data sets
- Greater understanding of efficient conjoint and choice designs using concepts of level balance, level overlap, orthogonality, and utility balance
- Statistical Analysis System (SAS) routines for the design of discrete choice plans using computerized searches (Kuhfeld, Tobias, and Garratt 1994)
- Advances in the power and ease of use of market simulators offered both by commercial software developers and by consultants working with spreadsheet applications

The 1990s represented a decade of strong growth for conjoint analysis and its application in a fascinating variety of areas. Conjoint analysis had traditionally been applied to fast-moving consumer goods, technology products and electronics, durables (especially automotive), and a variety of service-based products such as cell phones, credit cards, and banking services. Other interesting areas of growth for conjoint analysis included design of Web sites, litigation and damages assessment, human resources and employee research, and Web-based sales agents for helping buyers search and make decisions about complex products and services. By the end of the decade, analysts had become so trusting of the technique that some used conjoint analysis to help them personally decide among cars to buy or members of the opposite sex to date.

4.4 Year 2000 and Beyond

Much recent research and development in conjoint analysis has focused on doing more with less: stretching the research dollar using IT-based initiatives, reducing the number of questions required of any one respondent with more efficient design plans and HB estimation, and reducing the complexity of conjoint questions using partial-profile designs.

Researchers have recently gone to great lengths to make conjoint analysis interviews more closely mimic reality: using animated three-dimensional renditions of product concepts rather than static two-dimensional graphics or pure text descriptions, and designing virtual shopping environments with realistic store aisles and shelves. In some cases the added expense of virtual reality has paid off in better data, in other cases it has not.

Since 2000, academics have been using HB-related methods to develop more complex models of consumer preference, relaxing the assumptions of additivity by incorporating noncompensatory effects, incorporating descriptive and motivational variables, modeling the interlinking web of multiple influencers and decision makers, and linking survey-based discrete choice data with sales data. Additional research includes efforts to customize discrete choice interviews so that they adapt to individual respondents in real time.

Interactive, customized discrete choice interviews can engage respondents in a dialog that probes their relevant decision space and reveals both compensatory (trade-off) and non-compensatory behavior (such as screening rules). It has long been held that buyers first screen available products to form consideration sets and then make choices within consideration sets. New research in adaptive CBC interviews has shown that staging the interview as a screening task (to select a consideration set) followed by focused trade-offs among considered products may lead to more accurate market simulation models, especially for high-involvement products and services described by many attributes (Gaskin, Evgeniou, Bailiff, and Hauser 2007; Johnson and Orme 2007).

Software developers continue to make conjoint analysis more flexible, as well as faster and less expensive to carry out. Software systems often support multiple formats, including paper-based, PC-based, Web-based, and hand-held-device interviewing. Developers keep a watchful eye on the academic world for new ideas and methods that appear to be reliable and useful in practice. Commercially available market simulators offer more actionable information as they incorporate price and cost data, leading to market simulations of revenues and profitability rather than just shares of preference.

To reduce the amount of manual effort involved in specifying successive market simulations to find better products, automated search routines are now available. These find optimal or near-optimal solutions when dealing with millions of possible product configurations and dozens of competitors—usually within seconds or minutes. This has expanded opportunities for academics working in the area of game theory. These academics can study the evolution of markets as they achieve equilibrium, given a series of optimization moves by dueling competitors.

Importantly, more people are becoming proficient in conjoint analysis as the trade is being taught to new analysts. Academics are including more units on conjoint analysis in business school curricula. A growing number of seminars and conferences are promoting conjoint training and best practices. And research is being published and shared more readily over the Internet.

On the horizon, advances in the fields of neuromarketing and neuroeconomics seem particularly relevant to conjoint analysis. Rather than directly ask respondents to rate or choose among product concepts, the response to conjoint stimuli may be simultaneously measured on multiple dimensions using brain imaging technology. Rather than building a single model of part-worth utilities to predict choice, researchers might develop different utility functions related to the ability of product characteristics to "light up" different areas of the brain associated with (for example) euphoria, memories, risks, rational decision making, and fears. Such studies could help marketers gain insight into the key drivers operating within the psyche that lead respondents to choose what they do. While this area seems promising, imaging technology is currently expensive and time-consuming, and the interpretation of brain image scans involves many assumptions and uncertainties (Page and Raymond 2006).

Yes, conjoint analysis is more than forty years old. But rather than stagnating in middle-age, it continues to evolve—transformed by new technology and methodologies, infused by new intellectual talent, and championed by business leaders. It is very much in the robust growth stage of its life cycle. In retrospect, very few would disagree that conjoint analysis represents one of the great success stories in quantitative marketing research.

Chapter 5

Choosing a Conjoint Method

It is paradoxical that many new developments in the conjoint analysis field have made the methods better than ever but have also made it more difficult to choose among methods. Limitations which earlier caused researchers to reject one flavor of conjoint analysis in favor of another have been overcome, thus blurring the lines of distinction between the approaches.

Conjoint analysis has become one of the most widely used quantitative tools in marketing research. When applied properly, it provides reliable and useful results. There are many conjoint methods. Just as the golfer doesn't rely on a single club, the conjoint researcher should weigh each research situation and pick the right combination of tools. It makes little sense to argue which method is the overall best approach. Each is designed to bring unique advantages to different research situations.

To get a feeling for the variety of conjoint analysis methods, consider the software packages offered by Sawtooth Software. Three primary systems are available: traditional full-profile conjoint analysis (also called conjoint value analysis or CVA), Adaptive Conjoint Analysis (ACA), and choice-based conjoint (CBC). These three software offerings are representative of the main trade-off approaches used in industry today. According to a survey of Sawtooth Software customers, the relative use of these approaches in the Sawtooth Software community is CVA (5%), ACA (13%), and CBC (82%) (Sawtooth Software 2008). See figure 5.1.

5.1 Traditional Full-Profile Conjoint Analysis

Sawtooth Software's version of traditional full-profile conjoint analysis is called CVA. Other software firms, including SPSS Inc. and SAS Institute, also offer traditional conjoint analysis systems. Full-profile conjoint has been a mainstay of the conjoint community for decades. Academics have suggested that the full-profile approach is useful for measuring up to about six attributes (Green and

---

Adapted from a paper entitled "Which Conjoint Method Should I Use?" published in the Fall 1996 issue of *Sawtooth Solutions*. Interest in the paper, along with a steady flow of new developments in the conjoint analysis field, led us to update the piece many times since its original publication.

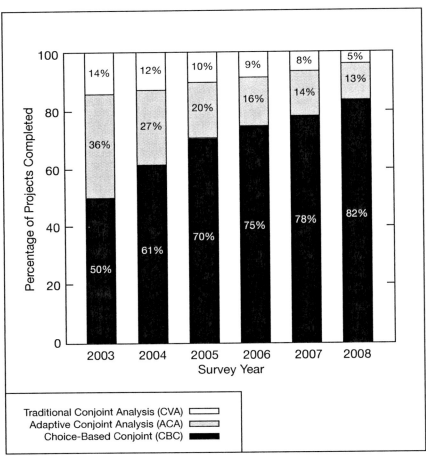

Source: Adapted from Sawtooth Software (2008).

Figure 5.1. Usage of Sawtooth Software conjoint methods

Srinivasan 1978). That number varies from project to project depending on the length of the attribute level text, the respondents' familiarity with the category, and whether attributes are shown as prototypes or pictures. Full-profile conjoint analysis may be used for paper-and-pencil studies, whereas ACA must be administered via computer. Full-profile conjoint can also be used for computer-assisted personal interviews (CAPI) and Internet surveys.

Through the use of composite attributes, traditional full-profile conjoint can measure interactions between attributes such as brand and price. Composite attributes are created by including all combinations of levels from two or more attributes. For example, two attributes each with two levels can be combined into a single four-level attribute. But interactions can only be measured in a limited sense with this approach. Interactions between attributes with more than two or three levels are better measured using CBC.

Sawtooth Software's CVA program can design pairwise conjoint questionnaires or single-concept card-sort designs. Showing one product at a time encourages respondents to evaluate products individually rather than in direct comparison with a competitive set of products. It focuses on probing the acceptability of a product offering rather than on the differences between competitive products. If a comparative task is desired, CVA's pairwise approach may be used. Another alternative is to conduct a card-sort exercise. Though respondents view one product per card, in the process of evaluating the deck, they usually compare them side-by-side and in sets.

Because respondents see the products in full profile (all attributes at once), they tend to use simplification strategies if faced with too much information to process. Respondents may key in on a few salient attributes and ignore the others (Gilbride and Allenby 2004; Hauser, Dahan, Yee, and Orlin 2006; Johnson and Orme 2007). Huber (1997) points out that buyers in the real world may simplify tasks when facing complex decisions for certain categories, so simplification is not, by definition, always a bad thing.

Other researchers have suggested that different respondents simplify in different ways, and the summary effect across respondents should reflect the aggregate behavior of real buyers. As a counterpoint, a recent study we conducted at Sawtooth Software showed that respondents who took more time in a CBC study produced significantly different choices (on aggregate) than respondents who answered the questionnaire quickly (Johnson and Orme 2007). This would suggest that simplification behavior by survey respondents is not innocuous. It is more likely that survey respondents who simplify and answer questionnaires rapidly are answering in ways that, at both the individual level and in the aggregate, are not entirely consistent with how they would behave in real-world choices.

5.2 Adaptive Conjoint Analysis

Released in 1985, Adaptive Conjoint Analysis (ACA) was Sawtooth Software's first conjoint analysis product. Other firms and academics have offered similar approaches, often referencing Sawtooth Software's product. ACA went on to become the most popular conjoint software tool and method in both Europe and the United States throughout the 1990s (Vriens, Huber, and Wittink 1997). Shortly after the turn of the century, CBC became more widely used—more on that later. ACA is user-friendly for the analyst and respondent alike. But ACA is not the best approach for every situation.

ACA's main advantage is its ability to measure more attributes than is advisable with traditional full-profile conjoint or CBC. In ACA, respondents do not evaluate all attributes at the same time, which helps solve the problem of information overload that plagues many full-profile studies. Some academics and researchers have written that respondents cannot effectively process more than about six attributes at a time in a full-profile task. This is a useful guideline, but there is much debate about this. The number of attributes that respondents can realistically manage in full profile depends on many factors, including the length of the attribute text, the use of graphics, and the respondents' sophistication and familiarity with the subject. ACA can include up to thirty attributes, although typical ACA projects involve eight to fifteen attributes. With six or fewer attributes, ACA's results are similar to the full-profile approach, though there is little compelling reason to use ACA in these situations.

In terms of limitations, the foremost is that ACA must be administered by computer. The interview adapts to respondents' answers as the survey progresses, which cannot be done via paper-and-pencil. Like most traditional conjoint approaches, ACA uses a main-effects model. This means that part-worth utilities for attributes are measured in an all-else-equal context, without the inclusion of attribute interactions. This can be limiting for studies in which it is important to estimate the price sensitivity for each brand. ACA has another limitation with respect to pricing studies: When price is included as one of the attributes, its importance is likely to be understated. The degree of understatement increases as the number of attributes studied increases. Recent studies have suggested that the importance of price can be understated by as much as two or three times, which is a significant problem (Pinnell 1994; Williams and Kilroy 2000).

ACA is a hybrid approach, combining stated evaluations of attributes and levels with conjoint pairwise comparisons. The first section of the interview employs a two-step self-explicated approach. Respondents rank or rate attribute levels (step 1), and then assign an importance to each attribute (step 2).

See exhibit 5.1 for an illustration of the ranking of attribute levels in terms of preference, which is step 1 of ACA. If Esprit were the most preferred designer and Liz Claiborne the least preferred, then the appropriate step 2 would be to ask the respondent for a rating of the importance of the difference between Esprit and Liz Claiborne, as illustrated in exhibit 5.2.

> *Rank these designers from most to least preferred.*
>
> > **Esprit**
> > **Liz Claiborne**
> > **Yves Saint Laurent**

Exhibit 5.1. ACA step 1: Rank attributes in terms of preference

> *If two designer dress suits were acceptable in all other ways, how important would this difference be?*
>
> **Esprit versus Liz Claiborne**
>
> *4 = extremely important*
> *3 = very important*
> *2 = somewhat important*
> *1 = not important at all*

Exhibit 5.2. ACA step 2: Rate importance of attributes

Which of these designer dress suits do you prefer?	
Liz Claiborne Polyester $375	Yves Saint Laurent Silk $425

1   2   3   4   5   6   7   8   9
Strongly   *Indifferent*   *Strongly*
prefer   *prefer*
left   *right*

Exhibit 5.3. ACA step 3: Pairs using graded rating scale

The self-explicated section of ACA puts emphasis on evaluating products in a systematic, feature-by-feature manner, rather than judging products as a whole or in a competitive context. The importance questions (step 2) are often challenging for respondents to answer reliably. Research presented at the Sawtooth Software conference suggested that dropping the importance questions from ACA surveys may result in better market share predictions and greater discrimination among attributes (as long as hierarchical Bayes is used to estimate the part-worths) (King, Hill, and Orme 2004). Subsequent analyses by Orme and Loke (2005) support these findings.

Using the information from the self-explicated section, ACA presents trade-off questions in the form of graded pairs. That is, two products are shown, and respondents indicate which is preferred using a relative rating scale. See exhibit 5.3 for an illustration.

The product combinations are tailored to each respondent to ensure that each is relevant and meaningfully challenging. Each of the products is displayed in partial-profile, which means that only a subset (usually two or three) of the attributes is shown for any given question. Because of the self-explicated introductory section, the adaptive nature of the questionnaire, and the ratings-based conjoint trade-offs, ACA is able to stabilize estimates of respondents' preferences for more attributes using smaller sample sizes than the other conjoint methods.

Huber (1997) states that pairwise comparisons reflect the sort of purchase behavior wherein buyers compare products side-by-side. ACA does well for modeling high-involvement purchases, in which respondents focus on each of a number of product attributes before making a carefully considered decision. Purchases for low-involvement product categories described by only a few attributes along with pricing research studies are probably better handled using another method.

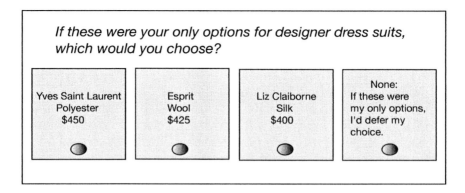

Exhibit 5.4. Choice set for designer dress suits

5.3 Choice-Based Conjoint

Choice-based conjoint analysis started to become popular in the early 1990s and lately has become the most widely used conjoint technique in the world (Sawtooth Software 2008). CBC interviews closely mimic the purchase process for products in competitive contexts. Instead of rating or ranking product concepts, respondents are shown a set of products in full profile and asked to indicate which they would purchase. Exhibit 5.4 shows a choice set for designer dress suits.

As in the real world, respondents can decline to purchase in a CBC interview by choosing *none*. If the aim of conjoint research is to predict product or service choices, it seems natural to use data resulting from choices.

There are many variations of CBC questionnaires. Rather than asking respondents to choose one from each set of product concepts, some researchers ask respondents to consider their next ten purchases, indicating how many of each product they would buy. This is known as chip allocation. Other researchers ask respondents to rank a full set of product alternatives or select the best and worst alternatives within each set. Most researchers favor the choice-based choose-one approach. It is not clear whether the additional effort of allocating choices or ranking (partial or complete) results in more accurate market-level models of buyer behavior, though it clearly increases the potential information content and respondent effort per completed task.

Pinnell (1999) has suggested that, rather than using allocation in CBC tasks, researchers can first ask respondents what occasions lead to different choices, and then ask respondents to make discrete choices based on different (and customized) occasion scenarios. For example, with beer purchases, people consume different brands depending on the consumption occasion (at home alone or at a party with friends). With breakfast cereal purchases, the choice depends on the individual in the family that will eat the cereal. And the prescription of medications by doctors depends on the characteristics of the patient. For these examples, separate models could be built based on the specific occasion, with the results weighted across models to predict overall shares of choice.

Huber (1997) argues that choice tasks are more immediate and concrete than abstract rating or ranking tasks. They ask respondents how they would choose, given a set of potential offerings. Choice tasks show sets of products, and therefore mimic buying behavior in competitive contexts. Because choice-based questions show sets of products in full-profile, they encourage more respondent simplification than traditional full-profile questions. Comparing CBC to traditional full-profile conjoint or ACA generally shows that attributes that are important get greater emphasis, and attributes that are unimportant get less emphasis.

Sawtooth Software offers a popular software program for CBC. Choice tasks can be administered via computer-assisted personal interviewing, telephone interviewing, Internet surveys, or paper-and-pencil questionnaires. Another leading software provider, SAS Institute, provides superb routines for the design of CBC experiments.

In contrast to either ACA or traditional full-profile conjoint (which automatically provide respondent-level part-worth preference scores), CBC results have traditionally been analyzed at the aggregate or group level. But with the availability of latent class and hierarchical Bayes (HB) estimation methods, both group- and individual-level analyses are accessible and practical. There are a number of ways to analyze choice results, the most popular of which are described below.

Aggregate Choice Analysis

Aggregate choice analysis was the first way to analyze data from choice-based conjoint studies. It was argued that aggregate analysis could permit estimation of subtle interaction effects (say, between brand and price) due to its ability to leverage a great deal of data across respondents. For most commercial applications, respondents cannot provide enough information with ratings- or sorting-based approaches to measure interactions at the individual level. While this advantage seems to favor aggregate analysis of choice data, academics and practitioners have argued that consumers have unique preferences and idiosyncrasies and that aggregate-level models that assume homogeneity cannot be as accurate as individual-level models.

Unless sophisticated cross-effects models are built, aggregate CBC analysis also suffers from its independence from irrelevant alternatives (IIA) assumption, often referred to as the red bus/blue bus problem. Very similar products in competitive scenarios can receive too much net share. Models that assume IIA fail when there are differential substitution effects across brands.

Latent Class Analysis

Latent class analysis addresses respondent heterogeneity in choice data. Instead of developing a single set of part-worths to represent all respondents (as in aggregate analysis), latent class simultaneously detects relatively homogeneous respondent segments and calculates segment-level part-worths. If the market is truly segmented, latent class analysis can reveal much about market structure (including group membership for respondents) and improve predictability over aggregate choice models. Subtle interactions can also be modeled with latent class analysis. To summarize, latent class analysis has the benefits of aggregate estimation while recognizing market heterogeneity.

Hierarchical Bayes Estimation

Hierarchical Bayes estimation (HB) offers a powerful way of borrowing information from every respondent in the data set to improve the accuracy and stability of each individual's part-worth estimates. It has consistently proven successful in reducing the IIA problem and in improving the predictive ability of both individual-level models and market simulation share results. HB estimation can employ either main-effects-only models or models that also include interaction terms. But researchers are finding that many, if not most, of the interaction effects that were discovered using aggregate CBC analysis were actually due to unrecognized heterogeneity (Orme and Heft 1999). So main-effects models with HB are often sufficient to model choice. I will explain this further.

Suppose we have individual-level part-worths in a data set, and there are two types of respondents. One group prefers Honda and is less price-sensitive; the other prefers Saturn and is more price-sensitive. If we perform sensitivity simulations with no interaction terms included, we will see that the demand or market share of Saturn changes more in response to price changes than the demand or market share of Honda. That is, respondents who initially prefer Saturn are more likely to switch to Honda due to price changes than vice versa. Even with no interaction terms included in HB models, a brand/price interaction can be revealed through market simulations. HB models can reflect between-group differences in price sensitivity.

If interactions occur principally within individual preference structures (a person's disutility for spending depends on the brand), then explicitly modeling interaction terms may be necessary for accurate share predictions. Which approach is appropriate for your situation—models that represent respondent heterogeneity or models with interaction terms—may be difficult to tell. The benefits of individual-level part-worths make a compelling argument for HB estimation. I have consistently seen HB estimation outperform aggregate logit in predicting shares for holdout choices and shares in actual markets, even when there is only modest respondent heterogeneity.

5.4   Partial-Profile Choice-Based Conjoint

Researchers that favor choice-based conjoint over ratings-based approaches have looked for ways to increase the number of attributes that can be measured effectively using CBC. One solution that has gained mixed support over the last few years is partial-profile CBC (Chrzan and Elrod 1995; Chrzan 1999). With partial-profile CBC, each choice question includes a subset of the total number of attributes being studied. These attributes are randomly rotated into the tasks, so across all tasks in the survey each respondent typically considers all attributes and levels.

The problem with partial-profile CBC is that the data are spread quite thin. Each task has many attribute omissions, and the response is the less informative (though more natural) choice among alternatives. As a result, partial-profile CBC requires larger sample sizes to stabilize results relative to ACA. Despite this shortcoming, some researchers who used to use ACA for studying many attributes have shifted to partial-profile CBC. The individual-level parameter estimates have less stability than with ACA. But if the main goal is to achieve accurate market simulations, some researchers are willing to accept larger standard errors in individual-level estimates.

Partial-profile CBC results tend to reflect greater discrimination among most and least important attributes relative to ACA. Though with the latest versions of ACA, one can probably remove this point of differentiation by omitting ACA's self-explicated importance questions. That is not to say that increased discrimination between attributes in terms of importance in conjoint is always the goal. But we do want to avoid artificial flattening due to self-explicated questions.

One obvious question that has not been resolved is whether partial-profile CBC is subject to the same price bias as ACA (i.e., understating price importance). We suspect that some of the price bias in ACA is due to the partial-profile nature of the process. Some early split-sample studies comparing partial- and full-profile CBC suggested that price bias was not a problem for partial-profile CBC. A number of more recent studies tend to point to lower price sensitivity estimates for partial-profile CBC compared to full-profile CBC.

Johnson, Huber, and Orme (2004) conducted a split-sample study that showed strong price bias for partial-profile choice. Another paper echoed this finding (Frazier and Jones 2004). Some researchers approach the problem of understating the importance of price by including price in each task and randomly selecting and ordering the remaining attributes. Including price in every choice task in partial-profile displays, however, does not necessarily resolve the concerns related to estimating price elasticity accurately using partial-profile choice. Recent studies suggest that price may still be understated even when included in each choice task.

5.5   Adaptive Choice-Based Conjoint

Newer CBC-related techniques combine the best aspects of adaptive interviewing with the realism and accuracy of choice data. Some researchers are first asking respondents about considered brands and features, and including just those within follow-up CBC exercises. Related to that, a new adaptive choice-based conjoint method (ACBC) proposed by Sawtooth Software offers a question flow that incorporates the well-established theory that buyers make complex choices by forming a consideration set (typically using cut-off rules) and then choosing a product within that consideration set. ACBC displays relevant products for respondents to consider by patterning them after the preferred product that respondents have first specified using a build-your-own (BYO) exercise.

Respondents find ACBC interviews more engaging, realistic, and relevant compared to traditional (static) CBC interviews. Even though the interviews are typically longer than standard CBC questionnaires, respondents generally prefer the overall experience. Sawtooth Software's ACBC questionnaire involves a progression of different-style choice exercises, which keeps things interesting. Plus, the products presented are centered around the respondent's preferred product concept, so they are more realistic and relevant. A handful of comparisons have been made between ACBC and standard CBC, and the part-worth utility results are generally quite similar (but not identical). ACBC captures more information at the individual level, often leading to more accurate predictions than standard CBC, even given smaller sample sizes for ACBC. Plus, the improved accuracy of individual-level preferences leads to better discrimination between respondents and more stable detection of useful market segments than standard CBC when applying common techniques such as latent class or cluster analysis.

ACBC does not seem to be a replacement for standard CBC. For smaller and more standard problems involving four or fewer attributes (such as the common brand-package-price research), standard CBC approaches perform admirably. But for problems involving seven to fourteen attributes, for example, the early research into ACBC is promising. Because it is such a new technique, it will take a few more years experience to learn the true value and place for ACBC. Sawtooth Software's ACBC is described more completely in chapter 12.

5.6   Which Conjoint Method Should You Use?

You should choose a method that adequately reflects how buyers make decisions in the marketplace. This includes not only the competitive context but also the way in which products are described in words and displayed with multimedia or physical prototypes. It also includes how products may be considered by respondents. Is the product in a high-involvement category for which respondents deliberate carefully on all features, or is it in a low-involvement category for which respondents simplify the choice task and choose almost intuitively?

If you need to study many attributes, ACA or possibly partial-profile CBC have traditionally been considered. But, especially over the last five years, the use of these approaches is waning. Partial-profile techniques are increasingly being viewed with suspicion, and researchers are generally displaying a greater amount of information in full profile within choice contexts. The traditional view that full-profile conjoint is limited to six attributes or fewer is being successfully challenged on a regular basis. Respondents seem to be able to deal with well-organized grids of information even better than early researchers and academics had supposed. Rather than try to limit respondents to comparing just two products at a time (to simplify the task), researchers are finding that respondents can often efficiently manage six or more product concepts at a time. And the resulting part-worth utilities tend to be better due to richer context. Displaying more rather than fewer product concepts per set often encourages respondents to reveal in-depth choice heuristics. In all cases, the number of attributes and product concepts we ask respondents to consider is a function of the amount of information that cleanly lays out on the page or computer screen.

In some areas of the world, survey populations do not have access to personal computers, and it may be too expensive to provide them. If your study must be administered by paper-and-pencil, this eliminates ACA or ACBC from consideration.

If you are dealing with small sample sizes (especially $n < 100$), you should be cautious about using CBC unless your attribute list is relatively concise and respondents are able to answer more than the usual number of choice questions. ACBC, ACA and traditional full-profile conjoint will stabilize estimates using smaller samples faster than CBC. See chapter 7 for a more complete discussion of sample size considerations.

For packaged goods research involving brand, package, and price, CBC with realistic store-shelf displays (often displaying dozens of product alternatives) is a robust approach. Increasingly, it is becoming hard to find reasons to prefer traditional ratings-based conjoint (CVA) or the ratings-based, partial-profile ACA method for general marketing research applications. CBC, as well as methods that leverage adaptive questioning and choice (such as ACBC), will dominate the conjoint landscape over the next decade.

For some projects, it may be difficult to decide which method to use. When you face a situation in which more than one conjoint approach seems appropriate, it is comforting to recognize that the methods, though different in approach, typically give quite similar results.

Chapter 6

Formulating Attributes and Levels in Conjoint Analysis

Defining proper attributes and levels is arguably the most fundamental and critical aspect of designing a good conjoint study. An attribute (sometimes called a factor) is a characteristic of a product (e.g., color), made up of various levels (there must be at least two for each attribute) or degrees of that characteristic (e.g., red, yellow, blue). The underlying theory of conjoint analysis holds that buyers view products as composed of various attributes and levels. Buyers place a certain part-worth utility on each of those characteristics, and we can determine the overall utility of any product by summing the value of its parts or levels.

In conjoint experiments, respondents express their preferences for products described by varying levels of attributes. By observing how respondents evaluate products in response to changes in attribute levels, we can estimate the impact each attribute level has upon overall product preference. That is, we can estimate utilities associated with attribute levels. After we learn respondents' preferences for the various attribute levels, we can predict how buyers might respond to a product with any potential combination of levels in our study, whether or not that actual product was displayed during the interview.

Typical full-profile conjoint studies in practice involve about eight or fewer attributes, each described on about two to five levels. Adaptive Conjoint Analysis (ACA) studies often include many more attributes, each also described on about two to five levels. Some attributes are nominal (e.g., color, brand), and we cannot know ahead of time whether respondents prefer one level over another. Some attributes are ordinal (e.g., expedited delivery versus normal delivery), and we know ahead of time that rational respondents would usually prefer the levels in a certain order. Other attributes, such as weight, speed, amount of money, or length of time, are quantitative in nature, with the order of levels determined by the attributes and objects being evaluated.

6.1 Present Appropriate Information

Attribute descriptions should be concise statements with concrete meaning. Avoid using ranges to describe a single level of an attribute, such as "weighs 3 to 5 kilos." Rather than leaving the interpretation to the respondent, it would be better to specify "weighs 4 kilos." Levels such as "superior performance" also leave too much in question. What does "superior performance" mean? Try to use specific language to quantify (if possible) the exact meaning of the level.

Attributes that cannot be adequately described in words should be represented in multimedia. But if attributes do not require multimedia to adequately communicate their properties, it would probably be a mistake to make them multimedia. Though a multimedia interview might seem more attractive to respondents, it might bias the results in favor of multimedia attributes.

Present just the right amount of information, neither too little nor too much. Some respondents have a difficult time dealing with more than about six to eight attributes in full-profile conjoint methods like CBC. When faced with too much information, respondents often resort to simplification strategies to deal with the difficulty of the task (Green and Srinivasan 1978). Unless respondents employ the same sort of simplification strategies when making real-world decisions, full-profile results may place too much emphasis on the few most important features.

6.2 Follow Guidelines in Defining Attributes

Attribute definition is central to conjoint study design. Assembling the right combinations of attributes and attribute levels is critical to the success of conjoint studies. This section provides guidelines for defining attributes and attribute levels for conjoint research. The guidelines apply to all varieties of conjoint analysis.

Cover the Full Range of Possibilities for Attributes

Attribute levels should cover the full range of possibilities for relevant existing products as well as products that may not yet exist, but that you want to investigate. A market simulator allows you to extrapolate and interpolate. Interpolation is likely to produce acceptable results, but extrapolation is prone to error and should be avoided. One way to ensure that you are including the appropriate levels and ranges is to ask your client to specify ahead of time the market simulations to be run during the analysis phase of your study. That exercise can often reveal weaknesses in your attribute specifications.

Use Independent Attributes

Attributes should be independent. This is especially important for partial-profile conjoint studies such as ACA and partial-profile CBC. With partial-profile or hybrid conjoint (ACA involves both), attributes that overlap in meaning can get "double counted," resulting in too much inferred influence on product choice. It is therefore important to economize; including attributes with overlapping meanings is wasteful.

Furthermore, levels for related attributes may not combine naturally with one another. Though it can lead to more realistic interviews, it is often detrimental and sometimes fatal to prohibit levels from occurring with others.

Define Mutually Exclusive Attribute Levels

Levels within each attribute should be mutually exclusive. This point becomes clear when you specify products using the market simulator (during the analysis phase) and are forced to associate only a single level from each attribute with each product definition. Consider the following attribute with three levels:

One Three-Level Attribute

Sunroof
Extended Warranty
Global Positioning System (GPS)

This formulation does not permit simulating preference for a car that has both a sunroof and a GPS. Similarly, we could not simulate preference for an automobile that had none of these features because there is no *none* level. There are two ways to resolve this quandary. We can create an attribute with all potential combinations of these features. This results in an eight-level attribute, if you include the option that none of these features is available:

One Eight-Level Attribute

Sunroof, Extended Warranty, GPS
Sunroof, Extended Warranty, No GPS
Sunroof, No Extended Warranty, GPS
Sunroof, No Extended Warranty, No GPS
No Sunroof, Extended Warranty, GPS
No Sunroof, Extended Warranty, No GPS
No Sunroof, No Extended Warranty, GPS
No Optional Features

Or we can formulate three separate attributes each with two levels as follows:

Sunroof
_____
No Sunroof
Sunroof

Extended Warranty
_____
No Extended Warranty
Extended Warranty

GPS
_____
No GPS
GPS

(Note that it is not necessary to state explicitly, for example, "No GPS." We could leave this level blank, so nothing would appear in that attribute position on the product profile.)

Creating an attribute with eight levels adds seven parameters to the model (see chapter 8 to understand why it is not eight) and forces the measurement of an explicit three-way interaction. With this more complex model definition, we can investigate whether there are diminishing returns (or unexpected synergies) by bundling the features. Splitting the options into three distinct binary attributes adds only three parameters if interaction parameters are not estimated.

Balance and Limit the Number of Attribute Levels

The number of levels you use to define an attribute can have a significant bearing on the results. The first concern has been called the number-of-levels effect (Currim, Weinberg, and Wittink 1981). All else being equal, attributes defined by more levels tend to get more importance. There is a large body of literature on this subject, and researchers recognize that both psychological and algorithmic effects play a role in the number-of-levels effect. The number-of levels effect is less problematic in ACA than full-profile conjoint methods such as CBC and traditional full-profile conjoint.

Ideally, you should try to balance the number of levels across attributes, especially for quantitative attributes such as price, speed, and weight. But there are situations in which some attributes in the real world (such as brand) have many more levels than other attributes. There is an argument for making the conjoint task mimic reality rather than balancing the number of levels and sacrificing realism. If in reality there are many more brands available on the shelf than package sizes, perhaps the same number-of-levels effect that influences conjoint analysis results also influences real world choices. Buyers may pay more attention to brand variation than to variation in other attributes.

Another guideline is that you limit the number of levels on which quantitative attributes are described. For most purposes, you should not need more than about five levels to describe attributes such as price or speed. It's usually better to have more data at each price point than to have thinner measurements at more price points. Measuring too many points along a quantitative function can result in imprecise part-worths and troublesome reversals. If you cover the entire range of interest with fewer levels, you can interpolate between levels within the market simulator to get finer granularity if needed.

6.3   Use Prohibitions Sparingly

When we impose prohibitions, we ensure that certain levels of one attribute never appear with certain levels of another attribute. Prohibitions or prohibiting pairs should be used sparingly or not at all. Specifying unnecessary or excessive prohibitions is a common mistake in conjoint studies.

The problem usually begins when the analyst or client notices that some product combinations displayed during the interview are not realistic, given what currently exists in the market. Sometimes a product is shown with all the best features at the lowest price, or two attribute levels that would not naturally occur in the real world are paired together. The inclination is simply to prohibit such combinations.

Researchers should exercise great restraint when considering prohibitions. Too many prohibitions, in the best case, can lead to imprecise utility estimation and, in the worst case, confounded effects and the complete inability to calculate stable utilities. It is better to prompt respondents that they will see combinations during the interview that are not yet available in the market or that seem unlikely. You can urge respondents to answer as if these products were actually available today.

There are other strategies for dealing with prohibitions. Consider an example with three brands of soda (e.g., Sawtooth Spritz, Kong Kola, and Martian Mist) and two package types (e.g., two-liter bottle or six-pack of twelve-ounce cans). Suppose that Martian Mist is only available in six-packs of twelve-ounce cans, and you are displaying actual pictures of the products, not potential products.

Rather than define a prohibition between Martian Mist and the two-liter bottle, it would make more sense to combine these two attributes into a single composite attribute with five levels, as illustrated in exhibit 6.1. Using the single-attribute approach, no prohibitions are required, but you will not be able to assess easily brand and package type as separate effects. This is probably not an issue if market simulations are used as the primary method of presenting results.

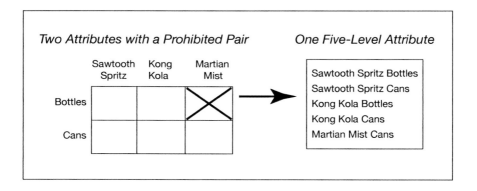

Exhibit 6.1. Resolving prohibitions with the composite-attribute approach

In the face of moderate to severe prohibitions, Adaptive Conjoint Analysis and other partial-profile conjoint methods are more robust than full-profile conjoint and full-profile choice-based conjoint methods. With full-profile methods, if two attributes have prohibited levels, the levels that appear for one attribute are necessarily correlated with the levels that appear for the other attribute. But with partial-profile methods, the two attributes do not always appear together within every conjoint question (one attribute may be missing). For such conjoint questions, those prohibitions have no effect, leading to relatively stable estimates of the levels for the two prohibited attributes.

Chapter 7

Sample Size Issues
for Conjoint Analysis

"I'm about to conduct a conjoint analysis study. How large a sample size do I need? What will be the margin of error of my estimates if I use a sample of only 100 respondents?" These are common questions. Unfortunately, they are difficult questions to answer because many issues come into play:

- What is it exactly that you are trying to measure to get a statistically significant result: a specific part-worth, preference for a product, or the difference in preference between groups of people?
- Do you expect that the differences between features/products/groups you are trying to detect are subtle or strong?
- What level of certainty do you need to be able to act upon your conclusions: 99% confidence, 90% confidence, or what?
- How large is the total population in the market for your product?
- What conjoint methodology do you plan to use? How many conjoint questions will each respondent answer?
- Do you need to compare subsets of respondents, or are you going to be looking at results only as a whole?
- How homogenous is your market? Do people tend to think alike, or are there strong differences in preferences among individuals?
- How do you plan to select your sample? Will it be a random sample or convenience sample?
- How large of a budget do you have for the project?

Answers to these questions play a role in determining the appropriate sample size for a conjoint study. This chapter provides advice and tools to help conjoint researchers make sample size decisions. It involves more statistical theory and formulas than other chapters, so please bear with me.

Though most of the principles that influence sample size determination are based on statistics, successful researchers develop heuristics for quickly determining sample sizes based on experience, rules-of-thumb, and budget constraints. Let us begin our discussion by making a distinction between sampling and measurement error. Subsequent sections will discuss each of these sources of error.

7.1   Sampling Error versus Measurement Error

Errors are deviations from truth. In marketing research we are always concerned with reducing error in cost-effective ways. Assuming that you have selected the appropriate modeling method, there are two main sources of error that cause preference data to deviate from truth. The first is sampling error.

Sampling error occurs when samples of respondents deviate from the underlying population. If we have drawn a random sample (each population element has an equal probability of being selected), sampling error is due to chance. If, on the other hand, our sample is not random (for example, a convenience sample), the sampling errors may be systematic. With random sampling, we reduce sampling error by simply increasing the sample size. With nonrandom sampling, however, there is no guarantee that increasing sample size will make the samples more representative of the population.

To illustrate sampling error, assume we wanted to figure out how far the average adult can throw a baseball. If we drew a random sample of thirty people, and by chance happened to include Ichiro Suzuki (outfielder for the Seattle Mariners), our estimate would likely be farther than the true distance for the average adult. It is important to note that the samples we use in marketing research are rarely random. Some respondents resist being interviewed and, by selecting themselves out of our study, are a source of nonresponse bias.

A second source of error in conjoint data is measurement error. We reduce measurement error by having more or better data from each respondent. Consider again the example of the baseball toss. Suppose you are one of the study participants. You throw the ball, but you accidentally step into an uneven spot on the ground, and the ball does not go as far as you typically could throw it. If we asked you to take another few tosses, and averaged the results, we would reduce the measurement error and get a better idea of how far you could throw a baseball.

In conjoint analysis, we reduce measurement error by including more conjoint questions. We recognize, however, that respondents get tired, and there is a limit beyond which we can no longer get reliable responses, and therefore a limit to the amount we can reduce measurement error.

7.2 Binary Variables and Proportions

Sampling error is expressed in terms of standard errors, confidence intervals, and margins of error. We can begin to understand what these terms mean by considering binary variables and proportions. In fact, we will spend a good deal of time talking about confidence intervals for proportions because the statistical principles can be applied to choice-based conjoint results and shares of choice in market simulations for all conjoint techniques.

A binary variable is a categorical variable with exactly two levels, such as a yes/no item on a consumer survey or a true/false checklist item. Many product attributes in conjoint studies have exactly two levels. And consumer choice itself is binary—to choose or not, to buy or not. Binary variables are usually coded as 1 for yes and 0 for no. Looking across a set of binary variables, we see a set of 1s and 0s. We can count the number of 1s, and we can compute the proportion of 1s, which is the number of 1s divided by the sample size n.

In statistical theory, the sampling distribution of the proportion is obtained by taking repeated random samples from the population and computing the proportion for each sample. The standard error of the proportion is the standard deviation of these proportions across the repeated samples. The standard error of a proportion is given by the following formula:

$$\textbf{standard error of a proportion} = \sqrt{\frac{pq}{(n-1)}}$$

where p is the sample estimate of the proportion in the population, $q = (1 - p)$, and n is the sample size.

Most of us are familiar with the practice of reporting the results of opinion polls. Typically, a report may say something like this: "If the election were held today, Mike Jackson is projected to capture 50 percent of the vote. The survey was conducted by the XYZ company and has a margin of error of ±3 percent." What is margin of error?

Margin of error refers to the upper and lower limits of a confidence interval. If we use what is known as the normal approximation to the binomial, we can obtain upper and lower limits of the 95% confidence interval for the proportion as

$$\textbf{margin of error for a proportion} = \pm 1.96 \sqrt{\frac{pq}{(n-1)}}$$

Going back to the polling report from XYZ company, we note that margin of error has a technical meaning in classical statistics. If XYZ were to repeat the poll a large number of times (with a different random sample each time), 95 percent of the confidence intervals associated with these samples would contain the true proportion in the population. But, of course, 5 percent of the confidence intervals would not contain the true proportion in the population. Confidence intervals are random intervals. Their upper and lower limits vary from one sample to the next.

Suppose we interview 500 respondents and ask whether they approve of the president's job performance, and suppose 65 percent say yes. What would be the margin of error of this statistic? We would compute the interval as follows:

$$\pm 1.96 \sqrt{\frac{(0.65)(0.35)}{(500 - 1)}} = \pm 0.042$$

The margin of error is ± 4.2 percent for a confidence interval from 60.8 to 69.2 percent. We expect 95 percent of the confidence intervals constructed in this way to contain the true value of the population proportion.

Note that the standard error of the proportion varies with the size of the population proportion. So when there is agreement among people about a yes/no question on a survey, the value of p is closer to one or zero, and the standard error of the proportion is small. When there is disagreement, the value of p is closer to 0.50, and the standard error of the proportion is large. For any given sample size n, the largest value for the standard error occurs when $p = 0.50$.

When computing confidence intervals for proportions, then, the most conservative approach is to assume that the value of the population proportion is 0.50. That is, for any given sample size and confidence interval type, $p = 0.50$ will provide the largest standard error and the widest margin of error. Binary variables and proportions have this special property—for any given sample size n and confidence interval type, we know the maximum margin of error before we collect the data. The same cannot be said for continuous variables, which we discuss in the next section.

7.3 Continuous Variables and Means

With continuous variables (ratings-based responses to conjoint profiles), one cannot estimate the standard error before fielding a study. The standard error of the mean is directly related to the standard deviation of the continuous variable, which differs from one study to the next and from one survey question to the next. Assuming a normal distribution, the standard error of the mean is given by

$$\textbf{standard error of the mean} = \frac{\textbf{standard deviation}}{\sqrt{n}}$$

And the margin of error associated with a 95% confidence interval for the mean is given by

$$\textbf{margin of error for the mean} = \pm 1.96 \left(\textbf{standard error of the mean} \right)$$

Suppose we had conducted an ACA study with forty respondent interviews. We want to estimate purchase likelihood for a client's planned product introduction with a margin of error of ±3 and a 95% confidence level. We run an ACA market simulation to estimate purchase likelihood on a 100-point scale, and the simulator reports the standard error next to the purchase likelihood estimate:

Total Respondents = 40

	Purchase Likelihood	Standard Error
Product A	78.34	3.06

The margin of error is ±1.96 × 3.06 = ±6.00, so we need to cut the margin of error in half to achieve our ±3 target level of precision. We know that the standard error of the mean is equal to the standard deviation divided by the square-root of the sample size. To decrease the standard error by a factor of two, we must increase sample size by a factor of four. Therefore, we need to interview about 40 × 4 = 160 or 120 additional respondents to obtain a margin of error of ±3 for purchase likelihood.

7.4 Small Populations and the Finite Population Correction

The examples we have presented thus far have assumed infinite or very large populations. But suppose that, instead of estimating the job performance rating of the president by the United States population at large, we wanted to estimate (with a margin of error of ±3 percent) the job performance rating of a school principal by members of the PTA. Suppose there are only 100 members of the PTA. How many PTA members do we need to interview to achieve a margin of error of ±3 percent for our estimate?

First, we introduce a new term: finite population correction. The formula for the finite population correction is $\frac{(N-n)}{(N-1)}$, where n is the sample size and N is the population size. The formula for the finite population correction is often simplified to $(1-f)$, where $f = \frac{n}{N}$, which is approximately equivalent to $\frac{(N-n)}{(N-1)}$ for all except the smallest of populations.

After a population reaches about 5,000 individuals, one can generally ignore the finite population correction factor because it has a very small impact on sample size decisions. Using the simplified finite population correction for a finite sample, the margin of error for a proportion and a 95% confidence interval is equal to

$$\pm 1.96 \sqrt{(1-f)\frac{pq}{(n-1)}}$$

The finite population correction may also be used for continuous variables and means.

With a population of 100, we can solve for n assuming an expected proportion. The worst-case scenario (i.e., the one that has the largest standard error) is for a 0.50 proportion, so it is standard to let $p = 0.50$. Solving for n, we discover that we would need to interview 92 PTA members, or 92 percent of the population to achieve a margin of error of ± 3 percent.

The important point to be made is that with small populations, you may have to interview a significant proportion of the population to achieve stable estimates. Suppose your client produces a very expensive, highly specialized piece of machinery, for which there were only 100 total potential customers in the world. Given many people's unwillingness to complete surveys, it will likely be much more difficult to complete surveys with 92 out of 100 potential buyers of this product than to interview, say, 1,000 potential buyers of something like office chairs, for which there are so many buyers as to approximate an infinite population. Even so, in terms of estimating a proportion, both scenarios lead to the same margin of error when projecting to the population of interest.

Conjoint studies may be used for large or small populations. We can use conjoint analysis for even the smallest of populations, provided we interview enough respondents to represent the population adequately.

7.5 Measurement Error in Conjoint Studies

Many researchers and dozens of data sets have demonstrated that conjoint utilities do a good job of predicting individual respondents' preferences for products. Holdout choice sets (choice tasks not used to estimate utilities) are often included in conjoint questionnaires. Using the conjoint data, a respondent's holdout choices usually can be predicted with a hit rate of roughly 75 to 85 percent. These choice tasks typically include between three and five different product concepts, so by chance we expect a success rate between 20 and 33 percent.

The hit rates with conjoint are significantly greater than chance and significantly better than the marketer's best guesses—even if the marketer knows each customer very well. In fact, conjoint predictions at the individual level frequently approach or sometimes even exceed test-retest reliability, suggesting that a good set of conjoint utilities is about as reliable at predicting choices to repeated holdout tasks as the respondents' earlier choices.

If there were only one buyer of your product in the world, you could learn a great deal about that individual's preferences from a conjoint interview. The utility data would be reasonably accurate for predicting his or her preferences and weights placed upon attributes. We can learn a great deal about an individual respondent provided we ask that respondent the right questions and enough questions. Let us consider numbers of conjoint questions or tasks needed for alternative methods of conjoint analysis.

Adaptive Conjoint Analysis

An Adaptive Conjoint Analysis (ACA) interview results in a set of utilities for each individual. We want conjoint measurements for each individual in the study to be as accurate as possible.

Of the three conjoint methods discussed in this chapter, ACA is the best at reducing measurement error. ACA's interviews adapt to the respondent, asking questions designed to be maximally relevant and efficient for refining utility estimates. The priors section helps in stabilizing the utility estimates at the individual level. One sees fewer reversals in part-worths (out-of-order utilities) for ordered attributes like price in ACA than in traditional conjoint and choice-based conjoint with individual estimation.

In ACA, one needs to decide how many pairs questions to ask. The number of pairs each respondent completes plays a significant role in reducing measurement error. The suggested number of pairs is $3(K - k - 1) - K$, where K is the total number of levels across all attributes and k is number of attributes. If respondents answer as many pairs as suggested, a total of three times the number of observations as parameters are available at the individual level for computing utilities (this includes information from the self-explicated priors). Sometimes the suggested number of pairs is greater than respondents can reasonably do. You should make sure not to overburden respondents because this can lead to poor results. You can ask fewer than the recommended number of pairs, though this increases the measurement error for each individual.

If your sample size is particularly small and the number of attributes to measure is large, ACA may be the best tool to use. In fact, it is possible to have an entire research study designed to learn about the preferences of one respondent, such as an important buyer of an expensive industrial product. As we discussed in chapter 5, there are many considerations for determining whether ACA is appropriate for a study. For further discussion of ACA measurement, estimation, and sample size issues, see Johnson (1987a).

Traditional Conjoint Studies

Like ACA, traditional full-profile conjoint (such as Sawtooth Software's CVA or SPSS's conjoint module) usually leads to the estimation of individual-level part-worth utilities. Again, the minimum sample size is one. But, because the traditional conjoint methodology does not include a self-explicated priors section, its utilities tend to have greater variability (larger standard errors) at the individual level relative to ACA (holding respondent effort equal).

One should include enough conjoint questions or cards to reduce measurement error sufficiently. Sawtooth Software's CVA manual suggests asking enough questions to obtain three times the number of observations as parameters to be estimated, or a number equal to $3(K - k + 1)$, where K is the total number of levels across all attributes and k is the number of attributes.

Respondents sometimes lack the energy or patience to answer many questions. We need to strike a good balance between overworking the respondent (and getting noisy data) and not asking enough questions to stabilize the estimates.

Choice-Based Conjoint

Though generally considered more realistic than traditional conjoint, choice-based questions are a relatively inefficient way to learn about preferences. As a result, sample sizes are typically larger than with ACA or traditional ratings-based conjoint, and choice-based conjoint (CBC) results have traditionally been analyzed by aggregating respondents. Lately, hierarchical Bayes has permitted individual-level estimation of part-worth utilities from CBC data. But to compute individual-level models, HB uses information from many respondents to refine the utility estimates for each individual. Therefore, one usually does not calculate utilities using a sample size of one. It should be noted, however, that logit analysis can be run at the individual level, if the number of parameters to be estimated is small, the design is highly efficient, and the number of tasks is large.

There are rules-of-thumb for determining sample sizes for CBC if we are willing to assume aggregate estimation of effects. Like proportions, choices reflect binary data, and the rules for computing confidence intervals for proportions are well defined and known prior to collecting data.

Consider a design with three brands and three prices. Assume each person completes ten tasks, and each task displays three products (i.e., each brand and price occurs once per task). If we interview 100 respondents, each brand will have been available for choice

$$(100 \text{ respondents}) \times (10 \text{ tasks}) \times \frac{(3 \text{ concepts})}{(3 \text{ brands})} = 1,000 \text{ times}$$

Johnson and Orme (1996) looked at about twenty commercial choice-based conjoint data sets and determined that having each respondent complete ten tasks is about as good at reducing error as having ten times as many respondents complete one task. Of course, in the limit this suggestion is ridiculous. It does not make sense to say that having one respondent complete 1,000 tasks is as good as having 1,000 respondents complete one task. But, according to Johnson and Orme (1996) simulation results, if a researcher obtains data from three to four hundred respondents, doubling the number of tasks they complete is about as good (in terms of reducing overall error) as doubling the sample size. It makes sense from a cost-benefit standpoint, then, to have respondents complete many choice tasks.

Johnson, who is the author of Sawtooth Software's CBC System, has recommended a rule-of-thumb when determining minimum sample sizes for aggregate-level full-profile CBC modeling: set

$$\frac{nta}{c} \geq 500$$

where n is the number of respondents, t is the number of tasks, a is number of alternatives per task (not including the *none* alternative), and c is the number of analysis cells. When considering main effects, c is equal to the largest number of levels for any one attribute. If you are also considering all two-way interactions, c is equal to the largest product of levels of any two attributes (Johnson and Orme 2003).

Over the years, we have become concerned that practitioners use Johnson's rule-of-thumb to justify sample sizes that are too small. Some feel that they will have ample stability in estimates when each main-effect level of interest is represented across the design about 500 times. But 500 was intended to be a minimum threshold when researchers cannot afford to do better. It would be better, when possible, to have 1,000 or more representations per main-effect level.

7.6 Typical Sample Sizes and Practical Guidelines

The recommendations below assume infinite or very large populations. They are based on the theories above and our observations of common practices in the market research community:

- Sample sizes for conjoint studies generally range from about 150 to 1,200 respondents.
- If the purpose of your research is to compare groups of respondents and detect significant differences, you should use a large enough sample size to accommodate a minimum of about 200 per group. Therefore, if you are conducting a segmentation study and plan to divide respondents into as many as four groups (i.e., through cluster analysis) it would be wise to include, at a minimum, $4 \times 200 = 800$ respondents. This, of course, assumes your final group sizes will be about equal, so one would usually want more data. The stronger segmentation studies include about 800 or more respondents.
- For robust quantitative research where one does not intend to compare subgroups, I would recommend at least 300 respondents. For investigational work and developing hypotheses about a market, between thirty and sixty respondents may do.

These suggestions have to be weighed against research costs. There are difficult decisions to be made based on experience, the application of statistical principles, and sound judgment. If, after the fact, you find yourself questioning whether you really needed to have collected such a large sample size for a particular project, it is an interesting exercise to delete a random subset of the data to see how having fewer respondents would have affected your findings.

A thorough discussion of sampling and measurement errors would require more time and many more pages. The reader is encouraged to consult other sources in these areas. For statistics and sampling see Snedecor and Cochran (1989) and Levy and Lemeshow (1999). For measurement theory see Nunnally (1967).

Chapter 8

Traditional Conjoint Analysis with Excel

A traditional conjoint analysis may be thought of as a multiple regression problem. The respondent's ratings for the product concepts are observations on the dependent variable. The characteristics of the product or attribute levels are observations on the independent or predictor variables. The estimated regression coefficients associated with the independent variables are the part-worth utilities or preference scores for the levels. The R^2 for the regression characterizes the internal consistency of the respondent.

Consider a conjoint analysis problem with three attributes, each with levels as follows:

Brand	Color	Price
A	Red	$50
B	Blue	$100
C		$150

For simplicity, let us consider a full-factorial experimental design. A full-factorial design includes all possible combinations of the attributes. There are 18 possible product concepts or cards that can be created from these three attributes:

$$3 \text{ brands} \times 2 \text{ colors} \times 3 \text{ prices} = 18 \text{ cards}$$

Further assume that respondents rate each of the 18 product concepts on a scale from 0 to 10, where 10 represents the highest degree of preference. Exhibit 8.1 shows the experimental design.

We can use Microsoft Excel to analyze data from traditional conjoint questionnaires. This chapter shows how to code, organize, and analyze data from one hypothetical respondent, working with spreadsheets and spreadsheet functions. Multiple regression functions come from the Excel Analysis ToolPak add-in.

Card	Brand	Color	Price ($)
1	A	Red	50
2	A	Red	100
3	A	Red	150
4	A	Blue	50
5	A	Blue	100
6	A	Blue	150
7	B	Red	50
8	B	Red	100
9	B	Red	150
10	B	Blue	50
11	B	Blue	100
12	B	Blue	150
13	C	Red	50
14	C	Red	100
15	C	Red	150
16	C	Blue	50
17	C	Blue	100
18	C	Blue	150

Exhibit 8.1. Full-factorial experimental design

8.1 Data Organization and Coding

Assume the data for one respondent have been entered into an Excel spreadsheet, illustrated in exhibit 8.2. The first card is made up of the first level on each of the attributes: (Brand A, Red, $50). The respondent rated that card a 5 on the preference scale. The second card has the first level on brand and color and the second level on price: (Brand A, Red, $100). This card gets a 5 on the preference scale. And so on.

After collecting the respondent data, the next step is to code the data in an appropriate manner for estimating utilities using multiple regression. We use a procedure called dummy coding for the independent variables or product characteristics. In its simplest form, dummy coding uses a 1 to reflect the presence of a feature, and a 0 to represent its absence. The brand attribute would be coded as three separate columns, color as two columns, and price as three columns. Applying dummy coding results in an array of columns as illustrated in exhibit 8.3. Again, we see that card 1 is defined as (Brand A, Red, $50), but we have expanded the layout to reflect dummy coding.

To this point, the coding has been straightforward. But there is one complication that must be resolved. In multiple regression analysis, no independent variable may be perfectly predictable based on the state of any other independent variable or combination of independent variables. If so, the regression procedure cannot separate the effects of the confounded variables. We have that problem with the data as coded in exhibit 8.3, since, for example, we can perfectly predict the state of Brand A based on the states of Brand B and Brand C. This situation is called linear dependency.

To resolve this linear dependency, we omit one column from each attribute. It really doesn't matter which column (level) we drop, and for this example we have excluded the first level for each attribute, to produce a modified data table, as illustrated by exhibit 8.4.

Even though it appears that one level from each attribute is missing from the data, they are really implicitly included as reference levels for each attribute. The explicitly coded levels are estimated as contrasts with respect to the omitted levels, which are constrained to have a weight of 0.

	A	B	C	D	E
1	Card	Brand	Color	Price	Preference
2	1	1	1	50	5
3	2	1	1	100	5
4	3	1	1	150	0
5	4	1	2	50	8
6	5	1	2	100	5
7	6	1	2	150	2
8	7	2	1	50	7
9	8	2	1	100	5
10	9	2	1	150	3
11	10	2	2	50	9
12	11	2	2	100	6
13	12	2	2	150	5
14	13	3	1	50	10
15	14	3	1	100	7
16	15	3	1	150	5
17	16	3	2	50	9
18	17	3	2	100	7
19	18	3	2	150	6

Exhibit 8.2. Excel spreadsheet with conjoint data

Card	A	B	C	Red	Blue	$50	$100	$150	Preference
1	1	0	0	1	0	1	0	0	5
2	1	0	0	1	0	0	1	0	5
3	1	0	0	1	0	0	0	1	0
4	1	0	0	0	1	1	0	0	8
5	1	0	0	0	1	0	1	0	5
6	1	0	0	0	1	0	0	1	2
7	0	1	0	1	0	1	0	0	7
8	0	1	0	1	0	0	1	0	5
9	0	1	0	1	0	0	0	1	3
10	0	1	0	0	1	1	0	0	9
11	0	1	0	0	1	0	1	0	6
12	0	1	0	0	1	0	0	1	5
13	0	0	1	1	0	1	0	0	10
14	0	0	1	1	0	0	1	0	7
15	0	0	1	1	0	0	0	1	5
16	0	0	1	0	1	1	0	0	9
17	0	0	1	0	1	0	1	0	7
18	0	0	1	0	1	0	0	1	6

Exhibit 8.3. Excel spreadsheet with coded data

	S	T	U	V	W	X	Y
1	**Card**	**B**	**C**	**Blue**	**$100**	**$150**	**Preference**
2	1	0	0	0	0	0	5
3	2	0	0	0	1	0	5
4	3	0	0	0	0	1	0
5	4	0	0	1	0	0	8
6	5	0	0	1	1	0	5
7	6	0	0	1	0	1	2
8	7	1	0	0	0	0	7
9	8	1	0	0	1	0	5
10	9	1	0	0	0	1	3
11	10	1	0	1	0	0	9
12	11	1	0	1	1	0	6
13	12	1	0	1	0	1	5
14	13	0	1	0	0	0	10
15	14	0	1	0	1	0	7
16	15	0	1	0	0	1	5
17	16	0	1	1	0	0	9
18	17	0	1	1	1	0	7
19	18	0	1	1	0	1	6

Exhibit 8.4. Modified data table for analysis with Excel

8.2 Multiple Regression Analysis

Microsoft Excel offers a simple multiple regression tool (under Tools + Data Analysis + Regression with the Analysis Toolpak add-in installed). Using the tool, we can specify the preference score (column Y) as the dependent variable (Input Y Range) and the five dummy-coded attribute columns (columns T through X) as independent variables (Input X range). You should also make sure a constant is estimated; this usually happens by default (by not checking the box labeled "Constant is zero").

The mathematical expression of the model is as follows:

$$Y = b_0 + b_1(\text{Brand B}) + b_2(\text{Brand C}) + b_3(\text{Blue}) + b_4(\$100) + b_5(\$150) + e$$

where Y is the respondent's preference for the product concept, b_0 is the constant or intercept term, b_1 through b_5 are beta weights (part-worth utilities) for the features, and e is an error term. In this formulation of the model, coefficients for the reference levels are equal to 0. The solution minimizes the sum of squares of the errors in prediction over all observations.

A portion of the output from Excel is illustrated in exhibit 8.5. Using that output (after rounding to two decimal places of precision), the utilities (coefficients) are the following:

Brand	Color	Price
A = 0.00	Red = 0.00	$ 50 = 0.00
B = 1.67	Blue = 1.11	$100 = -2.17
C = 3.17		$150 = -4.50

The constant or intercept term is 5.83, and the fit for this respondent $R^2 = 0.90$. Depending on the consistency of the respondent, the fit values range from a low of 0 to a high of 1.0. The standard errors of the regression coefficients (betas) reflect how precisely we are able to estimate those coefficients with this design. Lower standard errors are better. The remaining statistics presented in Excel's output are beyond the scope of this chapter and are generally not of much use when considering individual-level conjoint analysis problems.

Most traditional conjoint analysis problems solve a separate regression equation for each respondent. Therefore, to estimate utilities, the respondent must have evaluated at least as many cards as parameters to be estimated. When the respondent answers the minimum number of conjoint cards to enable estimation, this is called a saturated design. While such a design is easiest on the respondent, it leaves no room for respondent error. It also always yields an R^2 of 1, and therefore no ability to assess respondent consistency.

SUMMARY OUTPUT

Regression Statistics	
Multiple R	0.94890196
R Square	0.90041494
Adjusted R Sq	0.85892116
Standard Error	0.94280904
Observations	18

ANOVA

	df	SS	MS	F	Significance F
Regression	5	96.4444444	19.2888889	21.7	1.2511E-05
Residual	12	10.6666667	0.88888889		
Total	17	107.111111			

	Coefficients	Standard Error	t Stat	P-value
Intercept	5.83333333	0.54433105	10.7165176	1.6872E-07
X Variable 1	1.66666667	0.54433105	3.06186218	0.00986485
X Variable 2	3.16666667	0.54433105	5.81753814	8.2445E-05
X Variable 3	1.11111111	0.44444444	2.5	0.0279154
X Variable 4	-2.16666667	0.54433105	-3.98042083	0.0018249
X Variable 5	-4.5	0.54433105	-8.26702788	2.6823E-06

Exhibit 8.5. Conjoint analysis with multiple regression in Excel

One can easily determine the number of parameters to be estimated in a traditional conjoint analysis:

$$\# \textbf{ parameters to be estimated} = (\# \textbf{ levels}) - (\# \textbf{ attributes}) + 1$$

Most good conjoint designs in practice include more observations than parameters to be estimated (usually 1.5 to 3 times more). The design we have featured in this chapter has three times as many cards (observations) as parameters to be estimated. These designs usually lead to more stable estimates of respondent utilities than saturated designs.

Only in the smallest of problems (such as our example with three attributes and eight total levels) would we ask people to respond to all possible combinations of attribute levels. Large full-factorial designs are not practical. Fortunately, design catalogs and computer programs are available to find efficient fractional-factorial designs. Fractional-factorial designs show an efficient subset of the possible combinations and provide enough information to estimate utilities.

In our worked example, the standard errors for the color attribute are lower than for brand and price (recall that lower standard errors imply greater precision of the beta estimate). Because color only has two levels (as compared to three each for brand and price), each color level has more representation within the design. Therefore, more information is provided for each color level than is provided for the three-level attributes.

Chapter 9

Interpreting the Results of Conjoint Analysis

Conjoint analysis provides various outputs for analysis, including part-worth utilities, counts, importances, shares of preference, and purchase likelihood simulations. This chapter discusses these measures and gives guidelines for interpreting results and presenting findings to management.

Before focusing on conjoint data, it is useful to review some fundamentals for interpreting quantitative data. The discussion of the nature of measurement scales follows the classic discussion of Stevens (1946), which has been adopted by numerous social scientists and business researchers. For current definitions and discussion, one can refer to a book on business statistics (Lapin 1993).

9.1 Nature of Quantitative Data

There are four general types of quantitative data:

- Nominal data. Here the numbers represent categories, such as (1=male, 2=female) or (20=Italy, 21=Canada, 22=Mexico). It is not appropriate to perform mathematical operations such as addition or subtraction with nominal data or to interpret the relative size of the numbers.
- Ordinal data. These commonly occur in market research in the form of rankings. If a respondent ranks five brands from best 1 to worst 5, we know that a 1 is preferred to a 2. An example of an ordinal scale is the classification of strengths of hurricanes. A category 3 hurricane is stronger and more damaging than a category 2 hurricane. It is generally not appropriate to apply arithmetic operations to ordinal data. The difference in strength between a category 1 and a category 2 hurricane is not necessarily equal to the difference in strength between a category 2 and a category 3. Nor can we say that a category 2 is twice as strong as a category 1 hurricane.

I would like to express special thanks to Rich Johnson for his contributions to this chapter in the section entitled "Price Elasticity, Price Sensitivity, and Willingness to Pay."

- Interval data. These permit the simple operations of addition and subtraction. The rating scales so common to market research provide interval data. The Celsius scale is an example of an interval scale. Each degree of temperature represents an equal heat increment. It takes the same amount of heat to raise the temperature of a cup of water from 10 to 20 degrees as from 20 to 30 degrees. The zero point is arbitrarily tied to the freezing point of distilled water. Sixty degrees is not twice as hot as 30 degrees, and the ratio 60/30 has no meaning.

- Ratio data. These data permit all basic arithmetic operations, including division and multiplication. Examples of ratio data include weight, height, time increments, revenue, and profit. The zero point is meaningful in ratio scales. The difference between 20 and 30 kilograms is the same as the difference between 30 and 40 kilograms, and 40 kilograms is twice as heavy as 20 kilograms.

9.2 Conjoint Utilities

Conjoint utilities or part-worths are scaled to an arbitrary additive constant within each attribute and are interval data. The arbitrary origin of the scaling within each attribute results from dummy coding in the design matrix. We could add a constant to the part-worths for all levels of an attribute or to all attribute levels in the study, and it would not change our interpretation of the findings.

When using a specific kind of dummy coding called effects coding, utilities are scaled to sum to zero within each attribute. A plausible set of part-worth utilities for fuel efficiency measured in miles per gallon might look like this:

Fuel Efficiency	Utility
30 mpg	-1.0
40 mpg	0.0
50 mpg	1.0

30 mpg received a negative utility value, but this does not mean that 30 mpg was unattractive. In fact, 30 mpg may have been acceptable to all respondents. But, all else being equal, 40 mpg and 50 mpg are better. The utilities are scaled to sum to zero within each attribute, so 30 mpg must receive a negative utility value. Other kinds of dummy coding arbitrarily set the part-worth of one level within each attribute to zero and estimate the remaining levels as contrasts with respect to zero.

Whether we multiply all the part-worth utilities by a positive constant or add a constant to each level within a study, the interpretation is the same. Suppose we have two attributes with the following utilities:

Color	Utility	Brand	Utility
Blue	30	A	20
Red	20	B	40
Green	10	C	10

The increase in preference from Green to Blue (twenty points) is equal to the increase in preference between brand A and brand B (also twenty points). However, due to the arbitrary origin within each attribute, we cannot directly compare values between attributes to say that Red (twenty utiles) is preferred equally to brand A (twenty utiles). And even though we are comparing utilities within the same attribute, we cannot say that Blue is three times as preferred as Green (30/10). Interval data do not support ratio operations.

9.3 Counts

When using choice-based conjoint (CBC), the researcher can analyze the data by counting the number of times an attribute level was chosen relative to the number of times it was available for choice. In the absence of prohibitions, counts proportions are closely related to conjoint utilities. If prohibitions were used, counts are biased. Counts are ratio data. Consider the following counts proportions:

Color	Proportion	Brand	Proportion
Blue	0.50	A	0.40
Red	0.30	B	0.50
Green	0.20	C	0.10

We can say that brand A was chosen four times as often as brand C (0.40/0.10). But, as with conjoint utilities, we cannot report that Brand A is preferred to Red.

9.4 Attribute Importance

Sometimes we want to characterize the relative importance of each attribute. We can do this by considering how much difference each attribute could make in the total utility of a product. That difference is the range in the attribute's utility values. We calculate percentages from relative ranges, obtaining a set of attribute importance values that add to 100 percent, as illustrated in exhibit 9.1. For this respondent who's data are shown in the exhibit, the importance of brand is 26.7 percent, the importance of price is 60 percent, and the importance of color is 13.3 percent. Importances depend on the particular attribute levels chosen for the study. For example, with a narrower range of prices, price would have been less important.

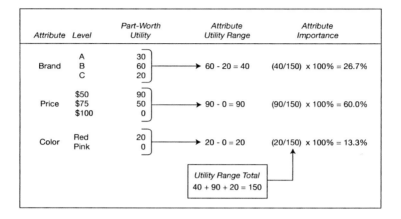

Exhibit 9.1. Relative importance of attributes

When summarizing attribute importances for groups, it is best to compute importances for respondents individually and then average them, rather than computing importances from average utilities. For example, suppose we were studying two brands, Coke and Pepsi. If half of the respondents preferred each brand, the average utilities for Coke and Pepsi would be tied, and the importance of brand would appear to be zero.

Importance measures are ratio-scaled, but they are also relative, study-specific measures. An attribute with an importance of twenty percent is twice as important as an attribute with an importance of ten, given the set of attributes and levels used in the study. That is to say, importance has a meaningful zero point, as do all percentages. But when we compute an attribute's importance, it is always relative to the other attributes being used in the study. And we can compare one attribute to another in terms of importance within a conjoint study but not across studies featuring different attribute lists.

When calculating importances from CBC data, it is advisable to use part-worth utilities resulting from latent class (with multiple segments) or, better yet, HB estimation, especially if there are attributes on which respondents disagree about preference order of the levels. (Recall the previous Coke versus Pepsi example.)

One of the problems with standard importance analysis is that it considers the extremes within an attribute, irrespective of whether the part-worth utilities follow rational preference order. The importance calculations capitalize on random error, and attributes with very little to no importance can be biased upward in importance. There will almost always be a difference between the part-worth utilities of the levels, even if it is due to random noise alone. For that reason, many analysts prefer to use sensitivity analysis in a market simulator to estimate the impact of attributes.

9.5 Sensitivity Analysis Using Market Simulations

Conjoint part-worths and importances may be difficult for nonresearchers to understand. Many presentations to management go awry when the focus of the conversation turns to explaining how part-worths are estimated or, given the scaling resulting from dummy variable coding, how one can or cannot interpret part-worths.

We suggest using market simulators to make the most of conjoint data and to communicate the results of conjoint analysis. When two or more products are specified in the market simulator, we can estimate the percentage of respondents who would prefer each. The results of market simulators are easy to interpret because they are scaled from zero to one hundred. And, unlike part-worth utilities, simulation results (shares of preference) are assumed to have ratio scale properties—it is legitimate to claim that a 40 percent share of preference is twice as much as a 20 percent share. Sensitivity analysis using market simulation offers a way to report preference scores for each level of each product attribute.

The sensitivity analysis approach can show us how much we can improve (or make worse) a product's overall preference by changing its attribute levels one at a time, while holding all other attributes constant at base case levels. We usually conduct sensitivity analyses for products assuming no reaction by the competition. In this way, the impact of each attribute level is estimated within the specific and appropriate context of the competitive landscape. For example, the value of offering a round versus a square widget depends on both the inherent desirability (utility) of round and square shapes and how many current competitors are offering round or square shapes. (Note that if no relevant competition exists or if levels needed to describe competitors are not included in the study, then it is possible to conduct sensitivity simulations considering the strength of a single product concept versus the option of purchasing nothing, or considering the product's strength in terms of purchase likelihood.)

Conducting sensitivity analysis starts by simulating shares of choice among products in a base case market. Then, we change product characteristics one level at a time (holding all other attributes constant at base case levels), We run the market simulation repeatedly to capture the incremental effect of each attribute level upon product choice. After we test all levels within a given attribute, we return that attribute to its base case level prior to testing another attribute.

To illustrate the method, we consider an example involving a study of mid-range televisions in 1997. The attributes in the study were as follows:

Brand

Sony
RCA
JVC

Screen Size

25-inch
26-inch
27-inch

Sound Capability

Mono Sound
Stereo Sound
Surround Sound

Channel Block Capability

None
Channel Blockout

Picture-in-Picture Capability

None
Picture-in-Picture

Price

$300
$350
$400
$450

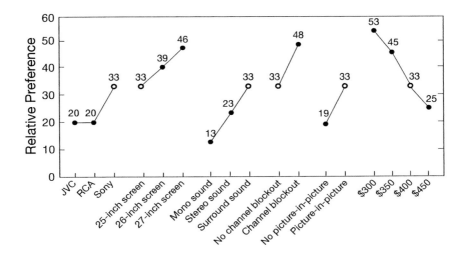

Figure 9.1. Results of sensitivity analysis

Suppose we worked for Sony and the competitive landscape was represented by this base case scenario:

Brand	Screen Size	Sound Capability	Channel Blockout Capability	Picture-in-Picture Capability	Price
Sony	25-inch	Surround	None	Picture-in-Picture	$400
RCA	27-inch	Stereo	None	Picture-in-Picture	$350
JVC	25-inch	Stereo	None	None	$300

Let us assume that, for this base case scenario, the Sony product captured 33 percent relative share of preference.

For a market simulation, we can modify the Sony product to have other levels of screen size, sound capability, channel blockout capability, and picture-in-picture capability, while holding the products from RCA and JVC constant. Figure 9.1 shows estimated shares of preference from this type of market simulation or sensitivity analysis. The potential (adjacent-level) improvements to Sony's product can be ranked as follows:

- Add channel blockout (48 relative preference)
- Reduce price to $350 (45 relative preference)
- Increase screen size to 26-inch (39 relative preference)

Sony cannot change its brand to RCA or JVC, so the brand attribute is irrelevant to management decision making (except to note that the Sony brand is preferred to RCA and JVC). And, although it is unlikely that Sony would want to reduce its features and capabilities, we can observe a loss in relative preference by including levels of inferior preference. One of those is price. Increasing the price to $450 results in a lower relative preference of 25 percent.

Before making recommendations to Sony management, we would, of course, conduct more sophisticated what-if analyses, varying more than one attribute at a time. Nonetheless, the one-attribute-at-a-time approach to sensitivity analysis provides a good way to assess relative preferences of product attributes.

9.6   Price Elasticity, Price Sensitivity, and Willingness to Pay

The results of conjoint analysis may be used to assess the price elasticity of products and services. It may also be used to assess buyer price sensitivity and willingness to pay. To begin this section, we should define price elasticity, price sensitivity, and willingness to pay:

- Price elasticity, by which we mean the price elasticity of demand, is the percentage change in quantity demanded divided by the percentage change in price. Price elasticity relates to the aggregate demand for a product and the shape of the demand curve. It is a characteristic of a product in a market.
- Price sensitivity is a characteristic of buyers or consumers. Some people are more sensitive to price changes than others, and the degree to which they are price sensitive can vary from one product or service to the next, one market to the next, or one time to the next. It can also vary with the characteristics of products described in terms of product attributes.
- Willingness to pay is a characteristic of buyers or consumers. A measure of willingness to pay shows how much value an individual consumer places on a good or service. It is measured in terms of money.

Conjoint analysis is often used to assess how buyers trade off product features with price. Researchers can test the price sensitivity of consumers to potential product configurations using simulation models based on conjoint results. Most often a simulation is done within a specific context of competitors. But when a product is new to the market and has no direct competitors, price sensitivity of consumers for that new product can be estimated compared to other options such as buying nothing.

The common forms of conjoint analysis measure contrasts between levels within attributes. The part-worths of levels are estimated on an interval scale with an arbitrary origin, so the absolute magnitudes of utilities for levels taken alone have no meaning. Each attribute's utilities are determined only to within an arbitrary additive constant, so a utility level from one attribute cannot be directly compared to another from a different attribute. To a trained conjoint analyst, an array of utilities conveys a clear meaning. But that meaning is often difficult for others to grasp. It is not surprising, then, that researchers look for ways to make conjoint utilities easier to interpret.

Monetary Scaling Trap

One common attempt to make conjoint utilities more understandable is to express them in monetary terms, or dollar equivalents. This is a way of removing the arbitrariness in their scaling. To do this, price must be included as an attribute in the conjoint design. Note that we cannot attach a monetary value to a single level (such as the color green), but must express the value in terms of differences between two colors, such as "green is worth $5 more than yellow." But if the attribute is binary (present/absent) such as "has sunroof" versus "doesn't have sunroof," the expressed difference is indeed the value of having the feature versus not having it.

The idea of converting utilities to dollar values can be appealing to managers. But some approaches to converting utilities to dollar equivalents are flawed. Even when computed reasonably, the results often seem to defy commonly held beliefs about prices and have limited strategic value for decision making.

Let us review a common technique for converting conjoint utilities to a monetary scale, and then we will suggest what we believe is a better approach. Here is how we can compute dollar equivalents from utilities. Imagine the following utilities for a single respondent for two attributes:

Attribute	Utility	Price	Utility
Feature X	2.0	$10	3.0
Feature Y	1.0	$15	1.0

For this respondent, a $5 change in price (from $15 to $10) reflects a utility difference of 2.0 (3.0 - 1.0). Therefore, every one utile change is equal to $2.50 in value (5 dollars/2.0 utiles). It then follows that feature X, being worth one utile more than feature Y, is also worth $2.50 more for this respondent.

We discourage the use of this type of analysis because it is a potentially misleading. Moreover, there is one practical problem that must be overcome if there are more than two price levels. Unless utility is linearly related to price, referencing different price points results in different measures of utiles per dollar. A common solution is to analyze the utility of price using a single coefficient. As long as the price relationship is approximately linear, this circumvents the issue.

Another problem arises when price coefficients are positive rather than negative as expected. This may happen for some respondents due to random noise in the data or respondents who are price insensitive. Such reversals would suggest willingness to pay more for less desirable features. One way to work around this is to compute dollar values of levels using average (across respondents) utilities, which rarely display reversals. Another approach to the problem is to ignore it, assuming that the reversals are just due to random noise. A more proactive way to avoid reversals is to use an estimation method that enforces utility constraints, though there are potential drawbacks to this approach (Johnson 2000).

Additional complications arise when the price coefficient for a respondent is extremely small in absolute value, approaching zero. In that case, the dollar equivalents for incremental features become very large, approaching infinity. A typical way to handle this is to characterize the centers of the distributions using medians rather than means.

This type of analysis assumes that the conjoint method has accurately captured respondents' price sensitivity. Some conjoint methods (ACA and potentially any partial-profile method) tend to understate people's price sensitivity. This can result in inflated willingness to pay values.

But after taking the appropriate steps to compute reasonable dollar equivalents, the results are potentially misleading. Even when accurate price sensitivity has been estimated for each individual, an examination of average values will often reveal that respondents are willing to pay much more for one feature over another than is suggested by market prices. This often causes managers to disbelieve the results. However, we'll demonstrate later that such outcomes are to be expected when the monetary value of levels is computed in this way.

There are a number of fundamental problems with analysis based on average dollar values. First, it attempts to ascertain an average willingness to pay for the market as a whole. Firms usually offer products that appeal to specific targeted segments of the market. The firm is most interested in the willingness to pay among its current customers, or among buyers likely to switch to its products, rather than in an overall market average. Second, this approach does not reference any specific product, but instead considers an average product. We expect that a respondent's willingness to pay for an additional feature would depend upon the specific product that is being enhanced (e.g., a discount or a premium offering). Third, and most fundamental, this approach assumes no competition. Because a product purchase usually constitutes a choice among specific alternatives, the competitive context is a critical part of the purchase situation. To illustrate the fallacy of interpreting average dollar values, without respect to competitive offerings, consider the following illustration.

Economics on "Gilligan's Island"

Though perhaps loathe to admit it, many have watched the popular 1960s American TV program *Gilligan's Island*. The program revolved around an unlikely cast of characters who became marooned on an uncharted desert island. Each episode saw the promise of rescue. And when it seemed that the cast was finally going to make it off the island, the bumbling Gilligan always figured out some way to ruin the day.

One colorful pair of characters were the ultrarich Mr. Howell and his wife. Now, imagine that one day a seaworthy boat with capacity for two passengers pulls into the lagoon and offers passage back to civilization for a price to be negotiated. What is the dollar value of rescue versus remaining on the island for Mr. and Mrs. Howell? Mr. Howell might pull out his checkbook and offer the crew millions of dollars. Under the assumption of no competition, the dollar equivalent utility of rescue is astronomically high. However, it might be much lower for other islanders of more limited means, and the average dollar value for all of them would have little relevance to the captain of the boat in negotiating a price. What would matter is the dollar value of the potential customers and no one else.

Now, assume, just as Mr. Howell and the first crew are preparing to shake on the deal, a second, equally seaworthy ship pulls into the lagoon and offers its services for a fixed $5,000. Ever the businessman, Mr. Howell will choose the $5,000 passage to freedom.

What has happened here? Is the utility of getting off the island for Mr. Howell suddenly different? Has his price sensitivity changed? No. The amount Mr. Howell would be projected to pay under the assumption of no competition is indeed very different from the amount he will pay given the appearance of another boat.

If the first boat's crew had administered a conjoint interview to Mr. Howell and had computed his willingness to pay under the first method reviewed in this article, they would have concluded that he was willing to pay a lot more than $5,000. But how meaningful is that information in light of the realities of competition? The realistic problem for the boat captain is to figure out what price the market will bear, given the existence of competitive offerings.

We can illustrate this point using another example. What is your willingness to pay for a color monitor for your laptop computer versus a monochrome screen? Assume we conducted a conjoint analysis including monochrome versus color monitors. If we computed your willingness to pay for color over monochrome, we would likely find that the incremental value of color over monochrome is worth a thousand dollars or more. But how meaningful is this information to a laptop manufacturer given the fact that laptops with color monitors are readily available on the market at quite inexpensive prices?

Price Sensitivity Simulations in Competitive Context

For most marketing problems involving competition, the best strategic information results from carefully defined market simulations. If a firm wants to assess the incremental demand resulting from offering specific features for its product, or improving its degree of performance, it should be estimated within a realistic competitive context.

Estimates of market demand should also be based on specific objectives. For example, the objective may be to determine how much more may be charged for a product or service by offering a new feature without any net loss in market acceptance. This approach involves simulating a realistic competitive scenario with a conjoint market simulator. Assume four products (A through D) represent the current relevant products in the marketplace. Further assume that the firm is interested in offering an additional feature for product A, and wants to estimate what new price can be charged while maintaining the same share of preference. We first simulate a base case with products A through D placed in competition with one another, where A does not include the new feature. We record its share of preference (say, 15 percent). We then conduct another simulation in which we improve A by offering a new feature (and hold the competition B through D constant). The share of preference for A should increase (say, to 20 percent). We then perform additional simulations (again holding competition constant) raising the price of the new product A until its share of preference again drops to the original 15 percent. The difference in price between the more expensive improved Product A that captures 15 percent and the old Product A that captured 15 percent reflects the incremental monetary value that the market will bear for the new feature, given the competitive context and the objective of maintaining share constant.

Market simulations conducted using individual-level utilities are best for this analysis. Individuals have different preferences, and the company that produces product A is most concerned with retaining current product A customers and attracting new buyers among those most likely to switch. The company does not care so much about individuals who are extremely unlikely to buy its offerings. Market simulations based on individual utilities support such complex market behavior, focusing the willingness-to-pay analysis on a relevant reference product and critical individuals rather than the market whole. Such market simulations can also reveal complex competitive relationships between products, such as degree of substitution (cross-effects) and differences in consumer price sensitivity to each product.

In summary, the common practice of converting differences between attribute levels to a monetary scale is potentially misleading. The value of product enhancements can be better assessed through competitive market simulations. If the market simulations are conducted using individual utilities, such simulations focus the price/benefit analysis on the customers that are most likely to purchase the firm's product(s) rather than on an overall market average. They provide strategic information based on a meaningful context that enables better decisions, while avoiding the pitfalls of other ways of analyzing data. Of course, the success of the simulation approach hinges on a number of assumptions, including the following: (1) the conjoint method produces accurate measures of price sensitivity, (2) the relevant attributes have been included in the simulation model, and (3) the relevant competitive offerings are reflected in the simulation model.

Chapter 10

Market Simulators
for Conjoint Analysis

The market simulator is usually considered the most important tool resulting from a conjoint analysis project. The simulator is used to convert raw conjoint (part-worth utility) data into something much more managerially useful: simulated market choices. Products can be introduced within a simulated market scenario and the simulator reports the percentage of respondents projected to choose each product. A market simulator lets an analyst or manager conduct what-if games to investigate issues such as new product design, product positioning, and pricing strategy. Market simulators are commercially available or can be constructed using spreadsheet programs.

10.1   What Is a Market Simulation?

A conjoint study leads to a set of utilities or part-worths that quantify respondents' preferences for each level of each attribute. These utilities can be analyzed in a number of ways. You can examine each respondent's utilities, but, if the number of respondents is large, this can be overwhelming. You might summarize the average utilities or compute average importances. You could create graphs and charts to display that information. But to many managers the results of conjoint analysis may seem abstract. Also, when we examine aggregate data or average responses, we may fail to detect important market segments—groups of consumers with unique and targetable preferences.

A good market simulator is like having all of your respondents gathered in one room for the sole purpose of voting on product concepts within competitive scenarios. The product concepts are defined in terms of the attributes and levels you used in the conjoint study. You walk into a virtual room, show them a market scenario (i.e., products A, B, and C), and they vote for the products they prefer. Millions of potential products and market situations could be evaluated, and your captive audience would never get tired, ask for lunch breaks, or require you to pay them by the hour.

How does a market simulator work? Let us suppose we were able to quantify how much people liked various flavors of ice cream. Let us refer to those preferences as utilities, and assume the following values for a given respondent:

Flavor	Utility	Price	Utility
Chocolate	0	$0.60	50
Vanilla	30	$0.80	25
Strawberry	40	$1.00	0

Using these utility values, we can predict how this respondent would choose between a vanilla cone for $0.80 or a strawberry cone for $1.00:

$$\text{Vanilla (30 utiles)} + \$0.80 \text{ (25 utiles)} = 55 \text{ utiles}$$

$$\text{Strawberry (40 utiles)} + \$1.00 \text{ (0 utiles)} = 40 \text{ utiles}$$

We predict that this respondent will prefer the vanilla cone.

Now suppose we had data for not just one, but 500 respondents. We could count the number of times each of the two types of cones was preferred, and compute a share of preference, also referred to as a share of choice. If 300 respondents choose the vanilla cone for $0.80 and 200 respondents choose the strawberry cone for $1.00, then we would obtain these shares of preference or choice:

Product Concept	Share of Choice
Vanilla at $0.80	$\frac{300}{500} = 0.60$
Strawberry at $1.00	$\frac{200}{500} = 0.40$

The simplest market simulation is a simulation that assumes a first-choice model. A first-choice model assumes respondents buy or choose the product alternative from the competitive set that has the highest total utility, as determined by summing the part-worth utilities associated with the levels describing each product. There are more sophisticated approaches for market simulations that are beyond the scope of this introductory chapter. These more advanced approaches include logit, Bradley-Terry-Luce, and randomized first-choice models.

10.2   Applications of Conjoint Simulations

Looking only at average preferences or part-worth utilities can mask important market forces caused by patterns of preference at the segment or individual level. Marketers are often not interested in averages, but in targetable segments or the idiosyncratic behavior of individuals.

Consider the following example with three respondents and their preferences or utilities for color:

Respondent	Blue	Red	Yellow
Manny	50	40	10
Moe	0	65	75
Jack	40	30	20
Average	30	45	35

Looking only at average utilities, we would pronounce that red is the most preferred color, followed by yellow. But if one of each color was offered to each respondent, red would never be chosen under the first-choice model, while yellow would be chosen once, and blue twice—the exact opposite of what aggregate utilities suggest. While this is a hypothetical example, it demonstrates that average utilities do not always tell the whole story. Many similar, complex effects can be discovered only through conducting simulations.

We can use simulators to answer basic questions about preference and shares of choice. We can use them to study the competitive environment and market segments. Furthermore, we can use the results of simulations to guide strategic decision making. Here are some of the benefits and applications of conjoint simulators:

- Conjoint simulations transform raw utility data into a managerially useful and appealing model: that of predicting market choice (share of preference) for different products. Under the proper conditions, shares of preference quite closely track with the idea of market share—something almost every marketer cares about.

- As demonstrated earlier, conjoint simulations can capture idiosyncratic preferences occurring at the individual or group level. These underlying effects can have a significant impact on preference for products in market scenarios. When multiple product offerings have been designed to appeal to unique segments of the market, capturing such effects is especially important for accurately predicting preference.

- Conjoint simulations can reveal differential substitutability (cannibalism or cross-elasticity effects) between different brands or product features. If two brands are valued highly by the same respondents (have correlated preferences), these brands will tend to compete more closely. Product enhancements by one of these brands will result in more relative share being lost by the correlated brand than by other, less similar brands within the same simulation. Examining aggregate utilities cannot reveal these important relationships.

- Conjoint simulations can reflect interaction effects between attributes. If the same respondents that strongly prefer the premium brand are also less price sensitive than those who are more likely to gravitate toward a discount brand, sensitivity simulations will reflect a lower price elasticity for the premium relative to the discount brand. A similar interaction effect can occur between many other types of attributes, such as model style and color.

- Conjoint simulators may be used to answer questions about new products and new product introductions. Given a current competitive environment, what product should I offer to maximize interest in my offering? How can I modify an existing product to capture more relative demand? A market simulator lets you input multiple products and place them in simulated competition with one another. Each product is defined using the attribute levels measured in the conjoint study (brands, colors, prices, speeds, warrantees, etc.). Therefore, if you have measured the relevant brands and features offered in the market, you can simulate a realistic market scenario within the market simulator. Within that market scenario, you can add a new product and see how well it competes. If the goal is to maximize share, offering the best features at the lowest price is often the trivial solution. The market simulator focuses on the demand side of the marketing equation; but it is also important to pay attention to the supply side and take the costs of producing different products/services into consideration. If you have cost information available to you, the market simulator permits you to investigate the incremental benefits of different features of a product relative to the cost of offering them.

- Conjoint simulators may be used to guide pricing strategy. What is the relative price sensitivity of different brands? If I raise my price by 10 percent, how will it affect my brand? How will it affect competitor's brands? You can conduct sensitivity analysis for attributes such as price using the market simulator to generate relative demand curves. The approach involves holding all other brands at a constant price and changing the price of a single brand, recording the relative share at each point for that brand along the price continuum.

- Conjoint studies can help us to answer questions about product bundles and product portfolios. What portfolio of products can I offer to appeal to different market segments and maximize overall share? If you have segmentation information (such as demographics or firmographics), you can investigate product formulations that appeal to different groups of respondents. It is likely that, by designing products that appeal uniquely to targetable segments, you can increase overall share for your product line or occupy a niche that is not currently being served.

The next three sections of this chapter will provide more detailed examples of applications, focusing upon introducing new products, estimating demand curves and elasticities, and designing products to appeal to market segments. For the examples in these sections you should assume the following three attributes, each with three levels:

Brand	Style	Price
A	X	$100
B	Y	$150
C	Z	$200

10.3 Introducing New Products

Let us assume that your company is interested in entering a market that currently consists of just two competitors. There are only three attributes that adequately describe the products and account for preference in the market: brand, style, and price. The two products are Mellow (Brand A, Style X, at $100) and Mild (Brand B, Style Y, at $200).

Your company has developed a new product called Middling that has Style Z. You think Middling may appeal to buyers, and you want to investigate its potential with respect to the two existing products. The first step, typically, is to simulate the existing market scenario. You use the market simulator to define the two existing products:

Product	Brand	Style	Price
Mellow	A	X	$100
Mild	B	Y	$200

Suppose a market simulation leads to the following shares of preference:

Product	Share of Preference
Mellow	64.3
Mild	35.7

In this simulation, we see that 64.3 percent of respondents preferred Mellow and 35.7 percent preferred Mild. Note that the buyers in the simulation are all assumed to choose a product, so the shares of preference across products in the simulation sum to 100 percent.

Let us assume that you have actual market share information about these two brands. You note that the shares reported above do not necessarily match the actual market shares. You accept this, however, recognizing that many factors influence market shares in the real world that cannot be captured through conjoint analysis. You are principally interested in relative preferences, assuming that the marketplace is an equal playing field (equal distribution, awareness, effectiveness of sales force, and equilibrium long-range demand).

In the second stage of this simulation example, we'll define a new scenario that includes your company's proposed product: Middling (Brand C, Style Z, $150. You add another product to your simulation specifications:

Product	Brand	Style	Price
Mellow	A	X	$100
Mild	B	Y	$200
Middling	C	Z	$150

Running the simulation again might lead to the following shares of preference:

Product	Share of Preference
Mellow	42.5
Mild	21.3
Middling	36.2

You note that Mellow is still the most preferred product, but that your product Middling is preferred to Mild. Like any market research statistics computed from samples, shares of preference are not estimated without error. It is common to estimate a confidence interval to get a feeling for the degree of uncertainty due to sampling and measurement error associated with a given share of preference. Let us assume that the standard error reported for Middling in the simulation above was 1.53. The 95% confidence interval is computed by adding plus and minus 1.96 times the standard error to the estimated share of preference. In this example, the 95% confidence interval is 36.2 plus and minus $(1.96)(1.53) = 3.0$ share points, or the interval [33.2, 39.2].

You next may ask yourself what price you would need to charge to capture the same relative preference as Mellow. To simulate this, you lower the price slightly for your brand. Many simulators include the ability to interpolate between levels (straight line interpolation), so you can investigate even the smallest of price changes. As a first step, you decide to lower the price to $130 for Middling (while holding the specifications for Mellow and Mild constant). The new simulated shares are as follows:

Product	Share of Preference
Mellow	39.2
Mild	19.0
Middling	41.8

You have overshot the mark (Middling's share exceeds Mellow's share), so you try a slightly higher price than $130 and run the simulation again. You make repeated attempts until Middling's and Mellow's shares are equal. Let us assume that after a few more attempts, you discover that the price that makes your company's offering match the share of preference of the market leader is $136. Another way of thinking about this finding is that your proposed product Middling commands a $136 - $100 = $36 premium over Mellow. Respondents are indifferent between Brand A and Style X at $100 and Brand C and Style Z at $136.

10.4 Estimating Demand Curves and Elasticities

We will build upon the previous example during this section. We have computed shares of preference for three products that were defined using the following attribute level codes:

Product	Brand	Style	Price
Mellow	A	X	$100
Mild	B	Y	$200
Middling	C	Z	$150

The shares of preference for the products, as defined above, were as follows:

Product	Share of Preference
Mellow	42.5
Mild	21.3
Middling	36.2

Let us assume that we wanted to estimate a demand curve for your company's offering: Middling, in the context of the current competition and prices. We do this through sensitivity analysis. Recall that we measured three distinct levels of price: $100, $150, and $200. Note that we have already computed the share of preference for Middling when it is offered at $150 (36.2). To estimate the demand curve for Middling, we will need to conduct two additional simulations: a simulation with Middling at the lowest price ($100), and a simulation with Middling at the highest price ($200). For each of these simulations, we'll hold the Mellow and Mild product specifications constant.

To estimate Middling's share at the lowest price ($100), we use the following product specifications:

Product	Brand	Style	Price
Mellow	A	X	$100
Mild	B	Y	$200
Middling	C	Z	$100

After running another simulation, we may observe the following shares:

Product	Share of Preference
Mellow	33.9
Mild	15.6
Middling	50.5

We record Middling's share (50.5), and proceed to the next step. To estimate Middling's share at the highest price ($200), we use the following product specifications:

Product	Brand	Style	Price
Mellow	A	X	$100
Mild	B	Y	$200
Middling	C	Z	$200

We run the simulation again, and the following shares are reported:

Product	Share of Preference
Mellow	49.2
Mild	26.9
Middling	23.9

From these three separate simulation runs, we have the information we need to plot a demand curve for Middling, relative to the existing competitors and prices. Assuming that Mellow and Mild are held constant at current market prices, the relative shares of preference for Middling at each of the price points within the measured price range are as follows:

Middling Price	Middling Share of Preference
$100	50.5
$150	36.2
$200	23.9

We have demonstrated how to estimate a demand curve for Middling, relative to the existing competitors at current market prices. If the goal is to estimate demand curves for all brands in the study, the usual procedure is to record the share for a brand at each price level while holding all other brands at the average or middle price. It is often interesting to plot these demand curves and look at the patterns of price sensitivity among brands and the different slope of the curves from one segment of the curve to the next. It is also common to want to characterize the degree of price elasticity using a single value, referred to as the price elasticity of demand:

$$E = \frac{\text{percentage change in quantity demanded}}{\text{percentage change in price}}$$

If the brand or product follows the law of demand, as most products do, price increases lead to decreases in quantity demanded, and the elasticity is negative. The larger the absolute value of the elasticity, the more price sensitive the market is with respect to that brand or product.

Using the midpoints formula, we can compute the average price elasticity of demand across the demand curve for Middling:

$$E = \frac{\frac{(q_2 - q_1)}{(q_1 + q_2)/2}}{\frac{(p_2 - p_1)}{(p_1 + p_2)/2}}$$

$$E = \frac{\frac{(23.9 - 50.5)}{(50.5 + 23.9)/2}}{\frac{(200 - 100)}{(100 + 200)/2}} = \frac{-0.715}{0.667} = -1.073$$

Another way to compute the average price elasticity of demand (which can be more accurate if more than two price points along the curve have been estimated) is the log-log regression. One takes the natural log of prices and shares and regresses the log of share on the log of price (you can do this within a spreadsheet). The resulting beta is the average price elasticity of demand.

As with all conjoint simulation results, the resulting elasticities from conjoint simulators must be interpreted bearing in mind some assumptions. In particular, the degree of noise within the conjoint data is particularly relevant. For example, if the respondents to the conjoint survey answered in a more haphazard way compared to buyers in the real world, the price elasticities estimated from conjoint simulations may be uniformly understated (too insensitive). Even if this is the case, the relative price sensitivities for brands are still useful.

10.5 Designing Products for Market Segments

Customizing products to appeal to target segments or even individuals is a common theme in marketing. Many companies dedicate significant resources to developing a portfolio of products that it hopes will appeal to unique segments. For line extensions, the challenge for any company is to design new products that take share from its competitors without stealing an unacceptable amount of share from products within its existing line.

One common approach to designing an effective line extension is to use the conjoint data to segment the market into latent (not observed) market segments (sometimes referred to as clusters) that have similar preferences. These segments are called latent because they are not simply delineated based on an explicit variable such as gender, income, or company size. Rather, the underlying segments are revealed through a statistical segmentation technique such as cluster analysis or latent class modeling. Segments are formed with the goal of maximizing the differences in preference between groups while minimizing the differences in preference within groups. Once these latent segments have been identified, one can profile them in terms of other variables in the survey (i.e., demographics, usage, or media habits).

If you have enabled your market simulator to select respondents for analysis by segment, this can further enhance the power of the tool. For example, let's assume that a cluster analysis revealed three relatively different segments for the hypothetical example we've been using.

By examining the part-worths and importances for each group, you can gain insight into the product features that might appeal to each. You also should bear in mind the size of each segment, as this represents its demand potential. Consider the part-worth utility preferences in exhibit 10.1.

Attribute Level	Segment 1 (n = 128)	Segment 2 (n = 283)	Segment 3 (n = 216)
Brand A	39	-51	-44
Brand B	5	39	-29
Brand C	-44	12	73
Style X	61	-52	-34
Style Y	-23	45	-9
Style Z	-38	7	43
$100	56	55	50
$150	7	2	6
$200	-63	-57	-56

Exhibit 10.1. Part-worth utilities across segments

We can study the part-worths to learn about the differences among the segments. We can also use these preferences to simulate market choices for the market scenario we had used previously to obtain shares of preference across segments. Note that the shares below do not match the shares reported for earlier examples in this chapter. Since these results are for illustration only, no significance should be attached to this difference.

Product	Brand	Style	Price
Mellow	A	X	$100
Mild	B	Y	$200
Middling	C	Z	$150

	Shares of Preference			
Product	Segment 1 (n = 128)	Segment 2 (n = 283)	Segment 3 (n = 216)	Total (n = 627)
Mellow	84.8	21.5	22.2	34.7
Mild	7.4	40.0	14.2	24.5
Middling	7.8	38.5	63.6	40.8

Let us assume your company produces Old Middling under Brand C with Style Z at $150. Your total share of preference is 40.8 percent. We see from the simulation by segment that yours is the most preferred product within segment 3, and the second-most preferred product in Segment 2. Mellow, the Brand A product, clearly dominates Segment 1, which is the smallest segment.

Let us assume that your company was interested in offering an additional product, call it New Middling. We could examine the table of part-worth preferences in exhibit 10.1 as a first step in formulating hypotheses about what additional product might be successful.

Starting in order, you may first consider Segment 1, but this segment does not seem to offer many opportunities for your brand. Brand A, offering Style X at a low price, has got this relatively small segment nearly wrapped up, and this segment does not seem very receptive to Brand C.

You next consider Segment 2, which seems to represent a better opportunity for your brand. It is a relatively large segment that prefers Mild under Brand B, but also seems receptive to the Brand C product, Old Middling. Note also that Segment 2 strongly prefers Style Y, but your company currently offers only Style Z. By offering a Style Y product, you might be able to convert some current Brand B customers from within Segment 2 to your product line.

You currently dominate Segment 3 and should probably not consider designing another product to appeal to this segment, since a good deal of the possible share to be gained from a new product would be taken from your existing product within that segment.

Let us simulate what happens if, in addition to your current product Old Middling (Brand C, Style Z, $150), you offer another product, New Middling (Brand C, Style Y, $200).

	Shares of Preference			
Product	Segment 1 ($n = 128$)	Segment 2 ($n = 283$)	Segment 3 ($n = 216$)	Total ($n = 627$)
Mellow	82.2	17.2	18.6	31.0
Mild	7.2	32.0	11.9	20.0
Old Middling	6.8	27.7	47.8	30.4
New Middling	3.8	23.1	21.7	18.7

The new product has somewhat cannibalized the existing product, reducing its share from 40.8 (see the previous simulation) to 30.4, but has resulted in a relative overall gain of [(30.4 + 18.7)/40.8] - 1 = 20 percent in preference.

For line extension simulations you conduct, the answer will likely not be so clear and the process not so direct as we've shown here. You'd certainly want to investigate other product configurations to make sure you weren't overlooking even better opportunities to enhance share. You would also want to consider the cost implications of different options for line extensions. Also, you would probably want to conduct sensitivity analysis for the new product with respect to price, to determine a strategic price point (given your costs and market share goals).

Viewing the preferences and shares by segment is not required in designing an effective line extension. However, viewing the separate market segments can help you more quickly recognize patterns of preference, size the different segments of the market, and thus more easily arrive at a good solution.

This exercise of viewing segment-based preferences and designing products to fill heterogeneous needs is a useful approach. However, it would seem more efficient to let an automated search algorithm find an optimal product or set of products rather than to proceed manually. There are commercial software programs available that use different algorithms to find optimal or near-optimal solutions, even when the search space is extremely large. These optimizers use a variety of search algorithms, including exhaustive search, hill-climbing procedures, and genetic algorithms. Genetic algorithm and other search plug-ins for Excel are available, allowing researchers to construct their own simulators with optimization. More information on simulations and optimization approaches is available within the monograph by Krieger, Green, and Wind (2005).

10.6   Simulation Methods and Sample Sizes

Part-worth utilities can be used within a choice simulator to predict preference for different product concepts in competitive scenarios. There are various simulation methods, including the simple first-choice (maximum utility rule) and the logit or Bradley-Terry-Luce model. First-choice simulations assume that each respondent can choose or vote for only one product and that one alternative captures 100 percent of the share for each respondent. Shares of preference under the first-choice rule are proportions.

In contrast, logit or Bradley-Terry-Luce models let respondents choose products in a probabilistic manner. Suppose there are three products in a market scenario. Representing a respondent's preferences with a probabilistic model might show choice probabilities (0.6, 0.3, 0.1), but the first-choice rule would represent the probabilities as (1, 0, 0). The probabilistic model captures more information from each respondent and yields more stable share estimates. The standard errors for share predictions from logit or Bradley-Terry-Luce simulations are always smaller than under the first-choice rule. Therefore, if you plan to use the first-choice model, you will need larger sample sizes to stabilize share-of-choice estimates relative to probabilistic simulation models.

10.7   Interpreting the Output of Market Simulators

Under very controlled conditions (such as markets with equal information and distribution), market simulators often report results that closely match long-range equilibrium market shares. However, conjoint utilities cannot account for many real-world factors that shape market shares, such as length of time on the market, distribution, out-of-stock conditions, advertising, effectiveness of sales force, and awareness. Conjoint analysis predictions also assume that all relevant attributes that influence share have been measured. Therefore, the share of preference predictions usually should not be interpreted as market shares, but as relative indications of preference.

Divorcing oneself from the idea that conjoint simulations predict market shares is one of the most important steps to getting value from a conjoint analysis study and the resulting simulator. While external-effect factors can be built into the simulation model to tune conjoint shares of preference to match market shares, we suggest avoiding this temptation if at all possible. No matter how carefully conjoint predictions are calibrated to the market, the researcher may one day be embarrassed by differences that remain. Also, using external effects often changes the fundamental properties of the original simulation model, such as the price sensitivities and substitution rates among products (Orme and Johnson 2006).

10.8   Multi-Store Simulators

The assumption of equal distribution is often responsible for the greatest differences between actual market shares and simulated shares of preference. Fortunately, there is a correct and straightforward simulation method for this problem. A multi-store simulator provides an appropriate way to account for an unequal distribution of products across the market without changing the products' original price sensitivities or substitution rates (Orme and Johnson 2006).

A multi-store simulator allows the researcher to specify, in the simplest case, the percentage of the regions/stores that carry each product. Superior implementations specify which products are available within each region/store and how much volume each region/store accounts for. Respondents are then randomly selected (with probability proportional to store volume) to make simulated visits to multiple stores on each of hundreds or thousands of occasions and to make choices among available products. If the respondent locations are known, we assign respondents to visit the applicable regional stores, rather than using a random process of assigning respondents to stores. The multi-store simulator is not just a tool for adjusting simulated shares to reflect better the availability of products across the market (and, in turn, market shares), but it is also a tool that more directly accounts for substitution effects by recognizing which products compete directly with one another (because they tend to be offered within the same regions/stores).

Chapter 11

Maximum Difference Scaling

Maximum difference scaling (MaxDiff) has experienced a recent surge in popularity, especially among analysts familiar with conjoint and choice analysis. The percentage of conjoint software users employing MaxDiff has grown from 8 percent in 2005 to 31 percent in 2008 (Sawtooth Software 2008). Presentations featuring MaxDiff have won best paper awards at recent marketing science conferences, including ESOMAR, the Advanced Research Techniques (ART) Forum, and the Sawtooth Software Conference.

MaxDiff is used for measuring the importance or preference within a list of items, such as product features, brands, advertising claims, product packaging, and job-related factors. It is meant to replace standard (and problematic) ratings questions, in which we ask respondents to rate items on (typically) a five-point scale.

Although MaxDiff, also known as best-worst scaling, is not technically a conjoint method, it is very similar. MaxDiff is easier to understand than conjoint analysis, involves fewer pitfalls, and is applicable to a wide variety of problems. But MaxDiff is not a substitute for conjoint.

11.1 Motivation for Maximum Difference Scaling

As researchers, we are constantly measuring the importance of or preference for things. The default approach has been the rating scale, often formatted as a grid, such as the one in exhibit 11.1.

The good news about grid-style ratings is respondents can answer them very quickly, often in about five seconds or less per item. Thus, respondents can provide data on dozens of product features or brands, while leaving time for more questions that we like to pack into questionnaires. But is this really good news? Should speed alone be the goal?

A key problem with standard ratings of importance is that people say that most things are very important or extremely important. From a data analysis perspective, we would prefer them to use the full breadth of the scale in a discriminating way, without having so many items rated at the extremes. We would like to be

How important are these aspects
of fast food restaurants to you?

Not at all important *Not very important* *Somewhat important* *Very important* *Extremely important*

Has clean eating area	O	O	O	O	O
Has clean bathrooms	O	O	O	O	O
Some health foods items on the menu	O	O	O	O	O
You get your food quickly	O	O	O	O	O
Staff are dressed professionally	O	O	O	O	O
Prices are very reasonable	O	O	O	O	O
Your order is always filled right	O	O	O	O	O
Has a play area for children	O	O	O	O	O
Food tastes wonderful	O	O	O	O	O
Restaurant gives generously to charities	O	O	O	O	O

Exhibit 11.1. Typical ratings grid

able to discover differences in importance across items for each individual and differences across segments of respondents for each item. Unfortunately, we often see little variability because the standard rating scale allows respondents to give lazy, non-discriminating answers.

But the problem is even more insidious than we have described so far. While some respondents tend to favor the upper end of the rating scale (yea-saying), others respondents may gravitate toward lower scale points (nay-saying). Moreover, some conscientiously use the full breadth of the scale while others concentrate on a narrow section of the scale. These tendencies are referred to as scale use bias, and they harm our ability to get an accurate measurement of preferences. Scale use bias can be problematic when comparing groups of respondents to determine which group is most interested in a particular product feature. Is the observed difference real or just an artifact of the groups' scale use tendencies? Those involved in international research should be concerned if different cultures use rating scales differently. Indeed, comparing average ratings across countries can pose significant challenges.

Some researchers encourage respondents to provide a wider variety of responses both within and between items by adding points to the rating scale. But with more scale points, respondents often react by shifting their answers to the left or right, continuing to use few of the available scale points (such as the tendency to use every fifth or tenth point on a 100-point scale). Researchers have also tried to counter scale use bias by normalizing data across respondents—zero-centering the data and equalizing the variances. The resulting standardized scores are a bit awkward to present to decision-makers because they have positive and negative values. Furthermore, these post-processing steps do not resolve the fundamental problems with traditional rating scales.

When considering fast food restaurants,
among the four attributes shown here,
which is the most important and least important?

Most Important		Least Important
O	*Prices are very reasonable*	O
O	*Your order is always filled right*	O
O	*Food tastes wonderful*	O
O	*Some health foods items on the menu*	O

Exhibit 11.2. MaxDiff question

To add to the problem of scale use bias, some cultures or segments of the population have a difficult time communicating strength of preference using values on a rating scale. This is especially true for children and individuals with little education. MaxDiff avoids these issues. No scale is presented to respondents. There are no scale labels to misinterpret, so scale use bias is irrelevant. People of all ages, cultural backgrounds, and educational levels find it natural to make choices. MaxDiff also capitalizes upon the fact that people find it easier to identify extremes than to discriminate among items of middling importance. Making choices is common to the human experience; rating scales are not. MaxDiff resolves many problems with traditional rating scales.

11.2 Efficient Data Collection Mechanism

With MaxDiff, we begin with a list of items or attributes (typically eight or more) and the desire to measure them on a common scale of importance or preference. In each MaxDiff question, respondents are shown just a few of the items (typically four to six items at a time). For each set of items, respondents pick the most and least important (or most and least preferred), as shown in exhibit 11.2.

Respondents typically complete about eight to twenty-four such questions. Across the questions, each item is seen many times by each respondent. The questions are designed carefully so that each item appears approximately an equal number of times. Furthermore, each item appears approximately an equal number of times with every other item.

Jordan Louviere, the inventor of the technique, originally called the method best/worst and later referred to it as maximum difference measurement. The latter label refers to the idea that respondents selecting the best and worst items are identifying the pair of items with the maximum difference in importance or preference among all possible pairings of items within the question.

MaxDiff captures a great deal of information per unit of respondent effort. Consider a MaxDiff questionnaire with four items per set (items A, B, C, and D). If the respondent says that A is best and D is worst, we can infer a number of relationships (inequalities) among those four items. We of course know that A (best) is preferred to D (worst). But, we also know that A is preferred to both B and C. Furthermore, we know that B and C are also preferred to D. The only unknown is how B compares to C. Thus, with just two clicks, the respondent has provided information regarding five of the six possible paired comparisons within the set:

$$A > B, A > C, A > D, B > D, C > D$$

It is easy to see why MaxDiff may be considered an efficient mechanism for obtaining paired comparison information. The method of paired comparisons has been a mainstay of preference research for well over fifty years. Recent research has shown that MaxDiff works better than the traditional method of paired comparisons for scaling multiple items (Cohen 2003).

11.3   Analysis of Maximum Difference Data

Two common ways to analyze MaxDiff data are counting analysis and score estimation. Score estimation is often done using techniques such as aggregate logit, latent class, and hierarchical Bayes (HB).

Counting Analysis: Best and Worst Percentages

If the questionnaire design is near-orthogonal (meaning each item is shown approximately an equal number of times with every other item in the study) one may compute the percentage of times respondents choose each item as best (most important) or worst (least important). These two measures should run essentially counter to one another—items chosen most often as best will be chosen least often as worst. Table 11.1 shows hypothetical percentage best and worst results for ten items dealing with aspects of fast-food restaurants.

Best-Worst Percentage Differences

A simple way to combine the information from best and worst judgments is to subtract the percentage of times an item is selected worst from the percentage of times it is chosen best. For example, if item j is selected best 40 percent of the time and selected worst 10 percent of the time, the combined score for item j is 40 minus 10, or 30 percent. The combined scores range from a maximum of 100 percent (for an item always chosen best) to a minimum of -100 percent (for an item always chosen worst). Scores greater than zero indicate that an item is more likely to be chosen best than worst, whereas negative scores indicate that an item is more likely to be chosen worst than best. One can display the resulting scores

Table 11.1. Best and worst percentages from counts

Restaurant Characteristic	Percent Best	Percent Worst
Clean eating area	38.6	11.0
Clean bathrooms	29.4	18.6
Health food items	19.9	25.1
Get food quickly	20.8	27.6
Dressed professionally	18.3	30.7
Reasonable prices	23.1	23.8
Get order right	24.6	22.5
Play area	19.5	27.9
Tastes wonderful	36.1	13.5
Gives to charities	19.0	30.9

using bar charts. Such bar charts may be used to compare across segments of the population. Hypothetical percentage difference scores for males versus females are shown in figure 11.1.

Estimated Scores

A more precise way to estimate item scores involves applying a statistical model, such as aggregate logit, latent class, or hierarchical Bayes estimation (HB). Deciding to apply a model rather than just counting choices has benefits beyond better precision. The latent class technique, for example, divides respondents into groups that have similar preferences (needs-based segmentation). Hierarchical Bayes analysis provides stable and accurate scores for each individual, whereas counting results for one individual would typically be a bit less precise (Orme 2009a).

As with counting analysis, model estimation can lead to separate scores or weights using information from best choices alone, worst choices alone, or composite scores from best and worst choices. Score estimation involves dummy coding similar to what we would use in conjoint analysis. And, as with conjoint analysis, estimated scores typically include both positive and negative values. Note that items with negative scores are not necessarily undesirable to respondents—negative scores mean that these items are less desirable than those with larger or positive scores. Table 11.2 shows estimated scores (based on an aggregate logit model) for the restaurant study.

Some researchers find it easier to rescale positive and negative scores on a zero-to-100 scale, as shown in table 11.3. (Note that we could have employed a similar rescaling with the combined counts in figure 11.1.)

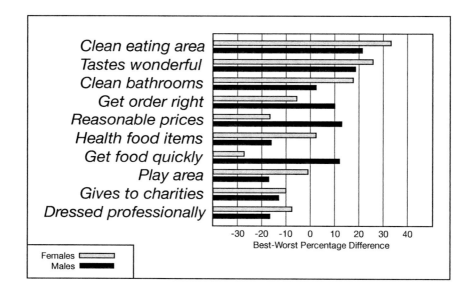

Figure 11.1. Combined importance scores by gender

Table 11.2. Scores from logit analysis (zero-centered scale)

Restaurant Characteristic	Importance Score
Clean eating area	1.30
Tastes wonderful	1.18
Clean bathrooms	0.80
Get order right	0.39
Reasonable prices	0.21
Health food items	-0.17
Get food quickly	-0.34
Play area	-0.56
Gives to charities	-1.32
Dressed professionally	-1.49

Table 11.3. Scores from logit analysis (zero-to-100 scale)

Restaurant Characteristic	Importance Score
Clean eating area	100
Tastes wonderful	96
Clean bathrooms	82
Get order right	67
Reasonable prices	61
Health food items	47
Get food quickly	41
Play area	33
Gives to charities	6
Dressed professionally	0

Table 11.4. Scores from logit analysis (100-sum scale)

Restaurant Characteristic	Importance Score
Clean eating area	25
Tastes wonderful	22
Clean bathrooms	15
Get order right	10
Reasonable prices	9
Health food items	6
Get food quickly	5
Play area	4
Gives to charities	2
Dressed professionally	2

Another approach is to place the weights on a ratio scale. With the ratio scale, all values are positive and an item with a score of 20 is twice as preferred as an item with a score of 10. We obtain ratio measures like this by taking the antilog of each item's zero-centered score and rescaling to a new score, so that the sum of the scores across all items is 100. In Microsoft Excel, the antilog formula is $=EXP(x)$, where x is the value to be transformed. After this transformation, all scale values are positive. It is common to rescale item scale values so their sum is 100, as shown in table 11.4. Other scale transformations may be used. For example, we could transform in a way that ensures that the average scale score across items is 100. Although ratio scales have strong properties, some researchers dislike the fact that the exponential transformation tends to stretch the scale so that a few best items receive large scores, while the worst items tend to group near zero.

Disaggregate Analysis

The illustrations in this chapter have involved aggregate (pooled) analysis. Most researchers analyze MaxDiff using disaggregate methods that estimate scores for segments using latent class analysis or scores for individuals using hierarchical Bayes models. In these cases, scores are developed separately for each segment or individual, with the scores averaged across segments or individuals to reflect the population.

An interesting outcome with disaggregate analysis that sometimes surprises researchers is that the summary importance scores for the population can modestly change in rank order depending on whether one averages across the raw individual-level scores from HB (or segment-based latent class analysis) or averages across the same scores transformed to the ratio scaling. The exponential transformation to the ratio (probability) scale cannot change the order of preference of items within the segment or individual. But, when averaging exponentially rescaled scores across segments or individuals, the resulting summary rank-order of preference can slightly change. For example, an item that appears fourth most important for the sample under the raw logit-based scaling may change to third or fifth in importance under ratio scaling.

11.4 Maximum Difference Scaling Versus Conjoint Analysis

Although there are many similarities between MaxDiff scaling and conjoint analysis, each method has unique characteristics. The most noticeable difference is that MaxDiff does not require a structured organization of attributes, each with two or more levels. We simply construct a list of items or attributes for measurement on a common scale. After we obtain scale scores, all items may be directly compared.

As with conjoint analysis, items in MaxDiff questionnaires can be prohibited from appearing with other items. But MaxDiff prohibitions are much less detrimental to obtaining stable score estimates than with conjoint analysis. We recently used simulated respondent data to test MaxDiff score estimation for an unrealistically large number of prohibited combinations and were impressed by the method's robustness. Recognize, however, that the simple method of counting analysis becomes less accurate when prohibitions are used. Model estimation with the statistical methods mentioned earlier is usually required to obtain proper scores when one imposes prohibitions.

Although one can use conjoint-looking attribute lists within MaxDiff, the method does not formally support a market simulation capability. MaxDiff is a method for prioritizing a list of items, placing them on a common preference or importance scale. Its focus is on contrasting items rather than learning how combinations of the items taken together (conjoined, as with conjoint) affect buyer preference for product wholes. As a result, the concept of adding scores to predict the desirability of a product made up of multiple features is not supported. That said, the inventor of the technique, Jordan Louviere, has claimed some success with MaxDiff in projecting preference for product concepts by adding the scores for their features. He has also used MaxDiff with attribute lists from conjoint analysis, calling it "best-worst conjoint." This approach to conjoint analysis has not gained traction or acceptance in the research community.

If the goal of the research is to understand and predict preference for product or service concepts made up of combined attributes, then conjoint analysis is appropriate. If the emphasis is on prioritizing a list of items or features, placing them on a common scale, then MaxDiff is preferred.

11.5   Concerns about Maximum Difference Scaling

A flexible and useful scaling technique, MaxDiff is not without its problems. Researchers note the following concerns:

- *MaxDiff surveys are long.* MaxDiff surveys are much longer than surveys using traditional ratings. The typical MaxDiff survey takes about three times as long to complete as a traditional ratings survey.
- *The information from "bests" may be different from "worsts."* Flipping the scores derived solely from "worst" judgments (by multiplying by -1) and comparing to those derived solely from "bests" can reveal statistically significant differences. That is not to say that the scores are substantially different from a managerial perspective or that they would lead to different recommendations. Generally, this lack of symmetry has been more of a concern to academics than to practitioners. A solution would be to drop the "worst" question from the MaxDiff questionnaire. But, to get the same amount of information, a best-only questionnaire would need to be much longer than a best-worst or MaxDiff questionnaire.
- *MaxDiff focuses equally on achieving stable estimates of both best and worst items.* Typically, managers are more concerned with discriminating among the top few (best) attributes. However, MaxDiff questionnaires focus equal attention on items at the extremes (both best and worst). Newer adaptive approaches to MaxDiff have been proposed that focus on obtaining stronger estimates of best items, while sacrificing a modest amount of precision for items near the bottom of the scale (Orme 2006).
- *There is controversy about MaxDiff's conforming to strict error theory.* Experts in statistics have argued that MaxDiff data do not formally conform to error theory consistent with logit analysis. Academics have argued this point, but practitioners have paid little attention. Logit scores are very consistent with respondent preferences observed via counting analysis, and, for practical purposes, there does not seem to be a problem in applying logit theory to MaxDiff. Researchers concerned about this technical point can obtain many of the benefits of MaxDiff by analyzing only the "bests" half of the MaxDiff questionnaire.
- *MaxDiff has an arbitrary scale origin.* The comparative nature of selecting a best and a worst item is a strength of MaxDiff, but it leads to a weakness—the scores have an arbitrary origin.

Suppose we ask two respondents to evaluate the importance of eight characteristics of airline travel. Of course, there are many more aspects than eight to describe the travel experience, but we have chosen to study just eight. For the first respondent, assume we have chosen the eight characteristics that he or she finds most important. For the second respondent, there may be other characteristics, many more important than the eight we have chosen to measure. That is, for these two respondents, the eight characteristics we have chosen differ in importance in an absolute sense. But there is no way to determine from their answers to MaxDiff questions that the first respondent values the eight characteristics more highly than does the second respondent.

With MaxDiff, we never ask respondents to indicate their feelings about the absolute importance of attributes. Rather, the data are relative in nature, and the scores reflect an arbitrary origin. Often, MaxDiff scale scores are zero-centered. It is also common to constrain a particular item score to be zero, with the other items scaled with respect to that zero score. Furthermore, if we transform to a zero-to-100 scale, we do not resolve the issue of an arbitrary scale origin. Only if we employ additional calibration questions can we give MaxDiff scores an absolute as well as a relative meaning. See Bacon et al. (2007), and Orme (2009b) for examples of this approach.

11.6 Predictive Validity

MaxDiff is more discriminating than standard ratings-based methods and, most importantly, is free from scale use bias. But enhanced discrimination is not the ultimate goal of item scaling. Rather, validity is paramount in terms of understanding buyers' true motivations, preferences, and, ultimately, in predicting their behavior.

Recent research comparing MaxDiff to standard ratings scales shows that MaxDiff is more accurate in predicting holdout choices and brand preferences than traditional rating scales (Cohen 2003; Chrzan and Golovashkina 2007). Because it is a relative newcomer, the evidence of MaxDiff's predictive validity is not as extensive as the evidence for conjoint methods' validity. MaxDiff has many elements in common with conjoint methods and has generated interest within the conjoint community. We expect further evidence of its usefulness and validity to be presented in upcoming conferences and publications.

Chapter 12

Adaptive Choice-Based Conjoint

Choice-Based Conjoint (CBC) is the most widely used conjoint technique today. The marketing research community has adopted CBC enthusiastically for several reasons. Choice tasks mimic what actual buyers do more closely than the ranking or rating tasks of traditional full-profile conjoint analysis. Choice tasks seem easy for respondents—everyone can make choices. And, equally important, there are solid statistical models for deriving part-worth utility estimates from choices.

Unfortunately, CBC is less informative than tasks involving ranking or rating of product concepts. Before making a choice, the respondent must examine the characteristics of, typically, three to six product concepts in a choice set, each described on multiple attributes. Yet, his or her choice reveals only which product is preferred, and nothing about strength of preference or the relative ordering of the non-preferred concepts.

Aware of the limitations of standard CBC, Johnson and Orme (2007) of Sawtooth Software introduced a new conjoint method—adaptive choice-based conjoint (ACBC). We can expect ACBC and related approaches to have a significant impact upon future conjoint practice. Adaptive methods are especially useful for studies involving five or more attributes.

12.1 Origins of Adaptive Choice-Based Conjoint

Despite its popularity as a method of marketing research, standard CBC has many limitations:

- Product concepts in many conjoint surveys are not close to the respondent's ideal. This can create the perception that the interview is not focused or relevant to the respondent.
- Respondents (especially in Internet panels) do choice tasks very quickly. We have observed that, after respondents warm up to a CBC task, they typically spend no more than twelve to fifteen seconds per choice set.
- To estimate part-worths at the individual level, we require each respondent to make many choices. But when a dozen or more similar choice tasks are

given to respondents, the survey experience is seen as repetitive and boring. Many respondents are less engaged in the process than the researcher might wish.

- Suppose a respondent is keenly intent on a particular level of a critical attribute (a *must have* feature), but there is only one such product available per choice task, then the respondent is left with two alternatives: select the product with the critical feature or select *none* (assuming the *none* option is available). Thus, for respondents intent on a few key levels of attributes, standard CBC choice tasks (featuring minimal level overlap) do not encourage respondents to reveal fully their product preferences. We learn only about a few *must have* features. To complicate matters further, superficial answers lead to seemingly consistent data and good statistical fit.

Many CBC respondents answer choice questions more quickly than would seem possible if they were giving thoughtful responses using an additive, compensatory model. Through the analysis of commercial CBC datasets, researchers have found that most respondent answers can be accounted for by simple screening rules involving a few attribute levels (Gilbride and Allenby 2004; Hauser et al. 2006; Johnson and Orme 2007). Combine this fact with the realization (by anyone who has answered a CBC questionnaire) that the experience seems repetitive and boring, and we are led to conclude that there is a need for a different way of conducting choice research.

Huber and Zwerina (1996) showed that choice designs are more statistically efficient when product alternatives within choice sets are nearly equal in utility. Their research gave rise to the term "utility balance." But choice tasks with utility balance cannot be designed without knowledge of the respondent's utilities, which is not available until after the interview. This chicken-and-egg problem has led to several attempts at adaptive methods, in which information from early choice tasks is used to create greater utility balance in later choice sets.

Early attempts at adaptive methods led to mixed results (Johnson et al. 2005). But these attempts relied upon the assumption that respondents use a simple additive/compensatory strategy, consistent with the logit rule. In the design of adaptive methods, we need to acknowledge the fact that respondents often ignore some attributes and rely on non-compensatory decision rules, such as screening based on a few *must-have* or *must-avoid* features.

How can we obtain better or more complete data from research participants, while preserving the simplicity of a choice task? Is it possible to devise a survey method that reduces respondent fatigue or boredom and acknowledges respondent use of non-compensatory rules, while providing sufficient information to estimate numerous attribute parameters?

12.2 A New Approach to Data Collection

Johnson and Orme (2007) proposed adaptive choice-based conjoint (ACBC) as a survey method to reflect more closely or mimic the purchase process and to encourage deeper thought processing from research participants. The goal was not to design choice tasks with the highest statistical efficiency, but rather to acquire better choice data.

Researchers have long recognized that buyers in high involvement categories deal with the complexity of choosing among potentially dozens or even hundreds of available products by first screening on key characteristics to develop a manageable consideration set. Then, to identify an overall winner within the consideration set, buyers typically weigh a wider variety of aspects as they evaluate the relative strengths and weaknesses of the considered products.

The Johnson and Orme (2007) approach recognizes that respondents employ screening rules. The approach asks respondents to make more detailed choices among product concepts that pass screening criteria. The aim is to encourage respondents to make choices more thoughtfully, much like they would in an actual purchasing situation.

The ACBC interview has several sections. Throughout the interview, there is an attempt to keep the respondent interested and engaged. The instructions appear on the screen in text, but as though they were spoken by a friendly interviewer. The image of an interviewer appears frequently at various places in the interview, from different perspectives and in different poses. The interviewer explains to the respondent that this is a simulation of a buying experience and gives a rationale for each interview section. See Sawtooth Software (2009) for an online ACBC interview about laptop computers.

Build-Your-Own Section

In the first section of the interview the respondent answers a build-your-own (BYO) questionnaire to introduce the attributes and levels, as well as to let the respondent design the product concept he or she would most likely purchase (given the attribute levels in the study). Past research has shown that respondents enjoy BYO questionnaires and answer them rapidly, and that the resulting choices have lower error levels than repetitive choices from standard CBC questionnaires (Johnson, Orme, and Pinnell 2006).

A screen for a BYO section of an interview about laptop computers is displayed in exhibit 12.1. Based on answers to the BYO questionnaire, the ACBC algorithm creates a pool of product concepts (around twenty-four to forty) that are near neighbors to the respondent's preferred product. Each concept in the pool is generated following a near-orthogonal design by altering a few of the attributes from the BYO-specified concept.

Please select the laptop computer you'd be most likely to purchase.
For each feature, select your preferred level.

Feature	Select Feature	Cost for Feature
Size:	○ 14 inch screen, 5 pounds (+ $750) ○ 15 inch screen, 6 pounds (+ $750) ○ 17 inch screen, 8 pounds (+ $1,000)	$ [＿＿＿]
Brand:	○ Acer ○ Dell ○ Toshiba (+ $50) ○ HP (+ $100)	$ [＿＿＿]
Processor:	○ Intel Core 2 Duo T5600 (1.86GHz) ○ Intel Core 2 Duo T7200 (2.00GHz) (+ $100) ○ Intel Core 2 Duo T7400 (2.16GHz) (+ $300) ○ Intel Core 2 Duo T7600 (2.33GHz) (+ $550)	$ [＿＿＿]
Operating System:	○ Vista Home Basic ○ Vista Home Premium (+ $50) ○ Vista Ultimate (+ $150)	$ [＿＿＿]
Memory:	○ 512 MB ○ 1 GB (+ $100) ○ 2 GB (+ $250) ○ 4 GB (+ $400)	$ [＿＿＿]
Hard Drive:	○ 80 GB ○ 100 GB (+ $50) ○ 120 GB (+ $100) ○ 160 GB (+ $150)	$ [＿＿＿]
Video Card:	○ Integrated video, shares computer memory ○ 128MB Video card, adequate for most use (+ $50) ○ 256MB Video card for high-speed gaming (+ $200)	$ [＿＿＿]
Battery:	○ 3 hour ○ 4 hour (+ $100) ○ 6 hour (+ $200)	$ [＿＿＿]
Productivity Software:	○ Microsoft Works ○ Microsoft Office Basic (Word, Excel, Outlook) (+ $150) ○ Microsoft Office Small Business (Basic + PowerPoint, Publisher) (+ $250) ○ Microsoft Office Professional (Small Bus + Access database) (+ $300)	$ [＿＿＿]
		Total $ [＿＿＿]

(Next)

Source: Adapted from Sawtooth Software (2009).

Exhibit 12.1. ACBC build-your-own questions

Screening Section

In the second section of the interview, the respondent answers screening questions in which product concepts (substantially like the one the respondent configured in the BYO stage) are shown a few at a time. Here, the respondent is not asked to make final choices, but rather to indicate whether each product concept is a possibility. Exhibit 12.2 displays a portion of the screening section for the laptop study. The exhibit shows only three product concepts, whereas an actual screening task might show four or five concepts on one screen.

The screening section identifies *must-haves* and *must-avoids* (unacceptables). After each group of concepts has been presented, previous answers are scanned to see if there is any evidence that the respondent is using non-compensatory screening rules. For example, we might notice that a respondent has expressed interest in only one level of an attribute, in which case the individual is asked whether that level is an absolute requirement (a *must-have*).

Past research with ACA has suggested that respondents are quick to mark many levels as unacceptable that are probably just undesirable. To avoid this possibility, ACBC offers only cutoff rules consistent with the respondent's previous choices and allows the respondent to select only one cutoff rule per screen. After each new screen of products has been evaluated, the respondent has an opportunity to add an additional cutoff rule. After a screening rule is confirmed by the respondent, any products in the pool that have not yet been evaluated but that fail to meet the cutoff criterion are automatically marked as non-possibilities and eliminated from further consideration.

Choice Tasks Section

In the third section of the interview the respondent is shown a series of choice tasks that present the surviving product concepts (those marked as possibilities). These are presented in groups of three (triples), as shown in exhibit 12.3. At this point in the survey respondents should be evaluating concepts that are close to their BYO-specified product, concepts that they consider as possibilities and that strictly conform to any cutoff, *must-have*, or *must-avoid* rules. To facilitate respondent information processing, attributes that are tied (have common attribute levels across the concepts) are grayed out, allowing respondents to focus on attribute differences across the concepts. Tied attributes are typically the most important factors for the respondent (based upon already established cutoff rules).

In the choice tasks section, then, the respondent is encouraged to discriminate further among products based upon features of secondary importance. Note that the approach of graying out tied attributes captures the benefits of partial-profile conjoint methods (only varying a subset of the attributes) but within the more realistic full-profile context.

Here are a few laptop computers you might like.
For each one, indicate whether it is a possibility or not.

Size:	15 inch screen, 6 pounds	15 inch screen, 6 pounds	14 inch screen, 5 pounds
Brand:	Toshiba	Dell	Dell
Processor:	Intel Core 2 Duo T7200 (2.00GHz)	Intel Core 2 Duo T7400 (2.16GHz)	Intel Core 2 Duo T7200 (2.00GHz)
Operating System:	Vista Ultimate	Vista Ultimate	Vista Ultimate
Memory:	4 GB	2 GB	4 GB
Hard Drive:	80 GB	160 GB	160 GB
Video Card:	128MB Video card, adequate for most use	Integrated video, shares computer memory	128MB Video card, adequate for most use
Battery:	3 hour	6 hour	4 hour
Productivity Software:	Microsoft Works	Microsoft Office Basic (Word, Excel, Outlook)	Microsoft Office Basic (Word, Excel, Outlook)
Price:	$1,550	$2,200	$1,800
	○ A possibility ○ Won't work for me	○ A possibility ○ Won't work for me	○ A possibility ○ Won't work for me

(Next)

Source: Adapted from Sawtooth Software (2009).

Exhibit 12.2. ACBC screening questions

Among these three, which is the best option? (I've grayed out any features that are the same, so you can just focus on the differences.)

Size:	15 inch screen, 6 pounds	15 inch screen, 6 pounds	17 inch screen, 8 pounds
Brand:	Dell	HP	Dell
Processor:	Intel Core 2 Duo T7200 (2.00GHz)	Intel Core 2 Duo T7200 (2.00GHz)	Intel Core 2 Duo T7200 (2.00GHz)
Operating System:	Vista Home Basic	Vista Home Premium	Vista Ultimate
Memory:	4 GB	4 GB	4 GB
Hard Drive:	160 GB	160 GB	160 GB
Video Card:	128MB Video card, adequate for most use	128MB Video card, adequate for most use	128MB Video card, adequate for most use
Battery:	4 hour	4 hour	6 hour
Productivity Software:	Microsoft Works	Microsoft Office Basic (Word, Excel, Outlook)	Microsoft Office Small Business (Basic + PowerPoint, Publisher)
Price:	$1,750	$1,500	$2,250
	○	○	○

(Next)

Source: Adapted from Sawtooth Software (2009).

Exhibit 12.3. ACBC choice task

In the choice tasks section, the winning concepts from each triple compete in subsequent rounds of choice tasks (as in a tournament) until the most preferred concept is identified. For example, if fourteen product concepts are considered as possibilities, it takes seven choice tasks, showing three concepts at a time, to identify the overall winner. A fourth section for calibrating a *none* utility threshold may be included, similar to the calibration section within an ACA survey.

12.3 Adaptive Versus Standard Choice-Based Conjoint

Johnson and Orme (2007) conducted two research projects comparing ACBC to standard CBC. A third study was reported by Orme and Johnson (2008). The first and third experiments were purely methodological projects, whereas the second involved a commercial study for a client.

ACBC was found to take from 50 to 300 percent longer than standard CBC, depending on the project and survey setup. This may appear to be a disadvantage at first, but it seems less so when one realizes that standard CBC questions are often answered in twelve to fifteen seconds after respondents are warmed up—seemingly inadequate time to provide thoughtful answers.

In the first and third studies reported by Johnson and Orme, respondents found the ACBC survey more engaging and less monotonous than standard CBC, even though the adaptive survey took longer on average to complete. The second study involved an abbreviated CBC questionnaire relative to ACBC, and respondents reported that the ACBC (at about triple the interview time on average) was more monotonous. In all three cases, respondents reported that the ACBC interviews were more realistic.

ACBC interviews provide more information than standard CBC interviews for computing part-worth utilities. Thus, ACBC has advantages over standard CBC when dealing with smaller sample sizes. Part-worth utilities may be estimated at the aggregate or segment level using standard multinomial logit methods. They may also be estimated at the individual level using hierarchical Bayes methods (Otter 2007).

Results from the Johnson and Orme studies showed that average part-worth utilities from standard ACBC and CBC were correlated at better than 0.90, indicating that the two approaches yield similar overall results. Evidence from predictive validity testing, however, suggested there are important differences between the methods (Johnson and Orme 2007; Orme and Johnson 2008).

Internal Validity

In terms of predictive validity, the ideal test would compare the ability of ACBC and CBC to predict real-world purchases. But, lacking real-world purchase data, Johnson and Orme measured predictive validity based on standard holdout CBC questions (Johnson and Orme 2007; Orme and Johnson 2008). At first blush, this may seem inappropriate. After all, if respondents use simplification strategies to answer repeated CBC tasks within market research surveys, why would one use similar tasks as the criterion for predictive validity? Also, using CBC-looking holdout questions would naturally favor the standard CBC approach.

Nonetheless, Johnson and Orme recognized that researchers were so accustomed to seeing methods compared based on CBC holdouts that they would expect to see the same method of evaluation for ACBC. But Johnson and Orme conducted their test of internal validity with a twist—their primary validity task involved comparing product concepts that were winners from earlier CBC tasks. Thus, if the respondent in the laptop computer study chose a Dell laptop in three preliminary CBC questions, the final task would ask the respondent to choose among three winning Dell laptops. This customized holdout choice task would be more difficult to predict than standard CBC holdout tasks because it would require information beyond strong brand preference for Dell alone.

In all three experiments, ACBC predicted respondents choices to the customized CBC holdout task more accurately than standard CBC. In other words, ACBC did better despite the bias in favor of CBC for such a comparison. The difference was statistically significant in the first and third tests (hit rates of 60.8 versus 50.0 and 44.3 versis 36.9), but nonsignificant in the second test (62.2 versus 59.5). The authors commented that the second test failed to include carefully controlled split-samples, so the results from the second test were not as robust (Johnson and Orme 2007; Orme and Johnson 2008).

External Validity

External validity is a more stringent and more valuable test of predictive validity than internal hit rates. For the first study reported by Johnson and Orme (2007), interviews of an additional 900 respondents were used to evaluate predictive validity. These holdout respondents completed twelve standard CBC tasks, and their data were not used to estimate part-worth utilities for the market simulation models.

Johnson and Orme (2007) found that the ACBC model was able to predict shares of choice for the holdout respondents as well as standard CBC (again, despite the bias in favor of CBC). But, when the holdout respondents were divided into three groups based on time spent completing the questionnaire, the authors found that ACBC did better at predicting the answers from respondents who took the most time to complete the interviews, and worse than CBC in predicting answers for respondents who took the least time to complete the interviews.

These results are consistent with the hypothesis that many CBC respondents use simple decision rules, such as choosing products that have a small number of critical attribute levels. It seems reasonable that holdout respondents who take longer with their choices may be using more elaborate and potentially more complex decision rules. To investigate this possibility, the authors tested whether slow and fast responders to the twelve holdout questions differed significantly with respect to part-worth utilities estimated from those tasks. A test for difference in parameters was statistically significant.

By the summer of 2009 more than fifty ACBC studies had been conducted by Sawtooth Software users. Many early adopters of ACBC have reported favorable results for ACBC when comparing predictions to actual market shares. Chapman et al. (2009) compared conjoint sales predictions with actual sales for personal computer peripherals, finding that predictions from ACBC were slightly better than predictions from standard CBC. Although the early evidence of predictive validity is positive for ACBC, it will take a number of years to determine whether the early enthusiasm about this technique is merited.

12.4 Summary and Conclusions

The ACBC method for collecting data provides several potential improvements over conventional CBC:

- ACBC seems to be a more faithful simulation of the buying experience, especially for high-involvement products.
- Respondents find the ACBC survey process to be more engaging than the standard CBC survey.
- ACBC can provide better predictions than standard CBC, especially for choices among preferred product concepts.
- ACBC may be superior to standard CBC when predicting choice shares for respondents who take longer and (presumably) are more thoughtful in completing a choice survey.

Most choice researchers admit that task simplification at the individual level exists, but many have believed that analyzing data from hundreds of respondents (each employing a distinct simplification strategy) should mitigate the problem. Choice researchers have argued that aggregate analyses accurately reflected the careful processing of information in real-world decisions.

Results from Johnson and Orme (2007), however, suggest that respondents who take more time to complete choice tasks are different from respondents who take less time to complete choice tasks. Aggregate analyses for these two groups are different. Furthermore, Johnson and Orme argue that a data collection technique that encourages greater depth of processing may produce more accurate share predictions.

There are some types of choice studies that may not be a good fit for ACBC. Brand-package-price studies, for which conventional CBC has been very popular and quite successful, would not seem to benefit from an adaptive approach. But for studies involving five attributes or more (especially in high-involvement contexts) an adaptive procedure offers compelling benefits.

Chapter 13

How Conjoint Analysis
Is Used in Industry

Since its introduction in the early 1970s, the use of conjoint analysis in commercial applications has grown exponentially. In a recent survey, Sawtooth Software (2008) asked its customers how many conjoint analysis projects they had conducted over the past year. Based on the responses, Sawtooth Software estimated that between 7,000 to 10,000 conjoint analysis projects were conducted over a twelve-month period by its customers alone. It is likely that well over 14,000 conjoint analysis projects are conducted worldwide per year when considering all the professionals that employ conjoint-related techniques.

As a powerful preference elicitation method, conjoint analysis has found use in a truly astounding variety of applications. Traditional uses include the following:

- Pricing research
- Product redesign/repositioning
- Line extension
- New product introduction
- Market segmentation
- Brand equity measurement

Here are a few additional applications I have read about or heard about firsthand from colleagues:

- Litigation (assessment of damages)
- Employee research (health plans, compensation packages)
- Online sales recommendation agents (collaborative filtering)
- Design of university curricula
- Capital budgeting
- Patient/physician communications

- Real estate planning and pricing models
- Advertising research
- Design of lotteries
- Job search/hiring
- Environmental impact studies
- Transportation planning

For this chapter, I have enlisted the help of a number of individuals using conjoint analysis in a variety of industry applications. These people have generously shared their perspectives regarding how conjoint analysis is used within their organizations. Their candor is greatly appreciated. Contributors' titles and affiliations are provided in appendix B.

13.1   Application of Choice Models at Procter & Gamble

Contributed by Greg Rogers

Like many consumer goods companies, Procter & Gamble (P&G) began using traditional conjoint methods to understand the importance of product and concept attributes. This was not always satisfying for the researcher, since only a limited number of ideas could be screened at one time. In addition, the "winning" result was often not practical to implement. The release of Sawtooth Software's Adaptive Conjoint Analysis package (ACA) in the mid-1980s helped address how many attributes could be tested, and generally made for relevant research, particularly in the area of new product development.

The dearth of pricing research techniques meant that P&G embraced discrete choice modeling for this purpose, as did many others in the industry. It was important to use choice-based conjoint instead of other methods, since, using this method, one could estimate the interaction of attributes—important if you expected different price sensitivities across items. In the early 1990s, many pricing research studies were fielded using DOS-based software packages. The number of discrete choice models run for pricing research has grown steadily in the past decade. Researchers have become more comfortable with the technique over time, with key advances in choice task presentation and analysis (namely hierarchical Bayes for estimating individual level utilities), making it the preeminent consumer research technique for measuring price sensitivity.

Pricing research is just one area where choice models are used at P&G today. Experiments in areas like new product forecasting and responsiveness to marketing media are proving that choice models are just coming into their own. A great many researchers now have familiarity with discrete choice models and are finding many applications.

13.2   Conjoint Analysis at Eastman Kodak

Contributed by Mike Lotti

Conjoint analysis is one of the marketing science tools that Business Research at Eastman Kodak Company has found to give practical, useful insights into product development and launch planning. It has enabled us to understand where to focus in the selection of feature sets, benefits, and setting an initial pricing strategy. For instance, a multinational choice-based conjoint exploration was instrumental in guiding the final configuration and pricing for the very successful launch of the series of EasyShare printer docks for Kodak digital cameras.

Successful use of conjoint methods requires careful implementation in two dimensions. Much attention is given to the statistical design of the task. We select the combinations of attributes and levels to ensure that managerially relevant effects can be estimated in the analytical model. We also ensure that there are sufficient participants to provide reliable parameter estimates. We can then gain insights into the patterns of choice, particularly at disaggregate levels.

However, it is also very important to account for the psychological aspects of the task. When dealing with a new technology not widely available in the market, we must ensure that the participants understand the relative merits of the choice options. The research manager must ensure that the participants can give valid responses. One approach is to sample "lead users" with the requisite knowledge. This can be effective if the sample can effectively represent the larger customer base. Another approach is to create familiarization tasks that allow the participants to learn about the benefits delivered by attributes and levels in the choice tasks. Either way, we want to ensure that the respondents are not "learning on the fly" and are not developing decision heuristics to simplify the task of sifting feature sets that they find confusing. A well-designed, well-implemented conjoint study is a vital tool in the research manager's kit.

13.3   Using Conjoint Analysis to Facilitate Doctor-Patient Communication

Contributed by Liana Fraenkel

Incorporation of patient preferences into medical decisions is essential to meet ethical standards, ensure patient satisfaction, increase compliance, and, ultimately, improve health outcomes. As patients become increasingly informed about medical illnesses and potential treatment options, it is imperative that we develop support systems that efficiently capture patients' perspectives.

The assessment of patient preferences shares similarities with the assessment of customer preferences for commercial products or services. When faced with complex treatment choices, patients, like consumers, must make complex trade-offs between competing attributes.

We have recently begun exploring the use of Adaptive Conjoint Analysis (ACA) as a possible decision support system to elicit patient values and treatment preferences. ACA is particularly attractive, because it is interactive and, therefore, permits inclusion of a substantial number of attributes without resulting in "information overload."

In our studies, we have shown that ACA is a feasible method to elicit patient treatment preferences in a reasonable amount of time (an average of eight to fourteen minutes). We have also demonstrated that patient treatment preferences may be driven by heuristics resulting in faulty decision making, and that patient preferences often conflict with physician prescribing behavior. Our long-term goal is to develop support systems based on ACA to improve medical decision making in clinical practice settings.

13.4   Conjoint Analysis at General Motors Corporation

Contributed by Jim Christian

General Motors (GM) has been using conjoint analysis since the early 1970s. Early conjoint models had relatively few variables and showed the importance of attributes such as fuel economy and quality. Later models gave us products such as the Cadillac Northstar engine, OnStar, XM Radio, Bumper to Bumper warranty, as well as many vehicles, such as the Chevrolet Avalanche. Conjoint has become an increasingly common methodology as advances in software and Internet methodology have resulted in dramatic decreases in study costs.

While complex market models may suffer from credibility issues at GM, the vast majority of conjoint conclusions have proven correct over time. We not only have extensive experience with these methods, but also routinely replicate conjoint findings using traditional research methods. We go to great lengths to ensure buy-in from our product teams before ever fielding a conjoint study. This emphasis on credibility also leads to one important source of validity problems: overeducation of respondents. Many times our teams want to use elaborate physical stimuli, test drives, and video to demonstrate the value of new vehicle features. Unfortunately, this level of education often cannot be duplicated in the marketplace. Overeducation can result in expensive vehicle features that customers are unwilling to pay for. Another significant validity issue involves the underestimation of price sensitivity in our models. That is to say that our models tend to overestimate the sales penetration of expensive vehicles and expensive vehicle features. We are hoping to correct for this latter problem by adjusting the price utilities based on past experience with similar conjoint models.

In central location studies, GM uses elaborate stimuli to provide credibility and ensure that respondents understand the attribute levels they are asked to evaluate. In general, we attempt to provide a level of education that is similar to that provided by our car dealerships and sales literature. Exterior design is often represented by full-size projected images. Interior dimensions are demonstrated in machines that change size and shape as a respondent sits in the "vehicle." Animated video presentations are often used to describe future technologies such as navigation systems. Finally, test drives and vehicle simulators are used to demonstrate dynamic attributes such as vehicle ride, handling, noise, and acceleration.

GM has also been working on methods to build very large conjoint models. One approach uses ratings of individual attribute levels to impute utilities for attribute levels that are not actually included in the choice questions. This self-explicated conjoint methodology has been used successfully to field complex studies over the Internet. Another method for building large conjoint models uses a central location study to field several choice interviews that together contain around sixty choice tasks. By breaking up a lengthy interview into smaller tasks, we have been able to maintain respondent motivation to construct very large conjoint models.

As the models become larger and optimal solutions are more difficult to identify, optimization software is being used increasingly to search across the billions of possible product portfolios. Manual analysis can be used to optimize one product with a few attributes. However, manual analysis will never find an optimal solution for problems that contain several products in one portfolio. Optimization software is used to automatically evolve the product attributes and identify solutions that optimize profit and/or estimated market share within a given set of constraints. After this automatic software identifies a diverse set of good solutions, manual analysis can again take over to identify even better solutions with other important characteristics (e.g., low risk, low investment, robust to scenario analysis, and good face validity).

GM fields conjoint research both as central location studies and as Internet studies. Our research-on-research shows that these two methods produce very similar conjoint models and product decisions. Central locations are generally preferred when physical stimuli must be used to ensure that respondents make informed decisions. However, physical stimuli can also make you vulnerable to overeducating the respondents. Central location studies also help to ensure research quality when the interview time must exceed forty-five minutes. On the other hand, Internet conjoint studies provide the critical advantages of low overall cost and a geographically representative sample. Climate-sensitive vehicle attributes, such as four-wheel drive, are known to be influenced by study location in the United States, and different countries exhibit even more differences.

As vehicle programs become increasingly global, GM would like to be able to field global conjoint studies over the Internet. To do this we need to make two things happen: (1) we need to establish international consumer panels with vehicle ownership identified and (2) we need to develop a shorter conjoint interview for use on the Internet. This shorter interview might use a combination of self-explicated and discrete choice conjoint methods.

13.5   Conjoint Analysis within Boeing Employees Credit Union

Contributed by Calvin Bierley

Boeing Employees Credit Union (BECU) is the fifth largest credit union in the United States, serving 385,000 members, largely in Washington State. BECU offers a full range of financial services.

BECU studied the preference for regular, insured savings versus money market accounts (MMA). BECU had long considered offering its membership a money market account (MMA) that would pay a higher interest rate as an alternative to a regular savings account. Research had shown that a large segment of the membership was risk averse and generally preferred the financial safety of a regular savings account that was federally insured, had no minimum balance requirement, and featured a guaranteed dividend rate. BECU did not want to introduce an MMA that was uninsured and required a minimum balance unless there was evidence that receiving a higher interest rate would compensate members for the more risky features of the MMA.

We used conjoint analysis to estimate the preference for an MMA versus a regular savings account. The trade-offs involved regular savings versus MMA, deposit insurance versus no insurance, various interest rates and balance requirements, $8 monthly fee versus no fees, and fixed versus variable interest rates on deposits. The results showed that deposit insurance, dividends, and fees were equally important, yet members were willing to trade deposit insurance and the no-balance requirement for a higher interest rate on their deposits.

Using the market simulator, we simulated these trade-offs to estimate the preference for the MMA versus regular savings. The simulations showed that the MMA was equally preferred to regular savings when the MMA paid a one-percentage-point-higher interest rate—even though the MMA required a $5,000 balance and the deposits were not federally insured. This suggested to us that there was sufficient demand for the MMA product. BECU decided to introduce the MMA to maintain and attract deposits during a period of low deposit interest rates and to preserve BECU's assets-to-reserves ratio, which is a key indicator of financial soundness monitored by regulators. BECU has offered an MMA at a higher dividend rate than regular savings since June 2004. The strong demand for the MMA predicted by conjoint simulations seems to be on target so far, since the actual percentage of deposits in MMAs versus savings accounts is already at 15 percent and steadily increasing.

BECU also studied a checking account option for designer checks. In the past, BECU had offered a limited variety of standard check designs without an additional menu of designer checks. Standard survey research and member comments showed that 43 percent of BECU members had previously purchased designer checks, which indicated a potential demand. However, a simple percentage for past usage did not tell us whether the demand for designer checks was likely to support the price required to break even. The unknown was how preference for designer checks would vary over prices ranging from $8 to $17 per box of checks while also varying the number of styles available from one to four.

We conducted a conjoint analysis study in which members made trade-offs among the designer check options, the price of the checks, and the number of available designer styles. The resulting market simulator indicated relatively high interest in designer checks. The preference for designer checks versus the standard option decreased from 60 to 30 percent over the price range. Offering four styles of checks instead of one supported a 10 percent higher share of preference at all price points. This suggested that there was a significant interest in designer checks even at the higher price range, and that offering more styles could further elevate the preference. BECU initially postponed offering designer checks until an economical arrangement could be made with a vendor to offer a large selection of check styles well in excess of the one to four styles used in the conjoint study. With moderate promotion and after less than one year, designer checks currently account for about 10 percent of all check orders, with an average price per order of $15. The prediction is that designer check usage will eventually double to 20 percent or more, as more members become aware of the availability of the designer check option. This is consistent with findings of the conjoint study that showed a 30 percent share of preference at $17 with greater value in having more check styles to choose from. The designer checks are a source of profits with a margin of $3.50 per order, whereas standard checks are priced at cost.

13.6   Adaptive Conjoint Analysis at the Canadian Department of Fisheries and Oceans

Contributed by Murray A. Rudd

The Canadian Department of Fisheries and Oceans (DFO) has a broad mandate to manage and protect the aquatic environment, facilitate sustainable marine development, maintain marine safety, and increase our understanding of oceans and aquatic resources in Canada. The Maritimes Region is responsible for the management of the Scotia-Fundy shelf, an area of highly diverse and valuable commercial fisheries.

Managing fishery resources in such a complex environment can be difficult, especially when the manager must make choices about where to direct scarce financial and human resources in a way that will best achieve policy objectives. One challenge is to understand how preferences may differ at various levels of government. Do the management decisions of resource managers reflect higher-level political directives and societal preferences? Are the operational-level priorities of enforcement officers in the field aligned with management priorities? If preferences are not aligned at different levels of the policy-management-enforcement chain, resource allocation may be, at best, inefficient.

The importance of preferences in government resource allocation problems suggests that stated preference surveys may be a valuable tool for identifying how efficient resource allocation decisions can be implemented. While discrete choice methods may be the preferred approach for assessing utility-theoretic consumer surplus using large samples, Adaptive Conjoint Analysis (ACA) may be the preferred survey tool for some specialized applications in which limited numbers of experts are queried about complex choices. Detailed resource allocation models will need detailed information about the preferences of a variety of groups within and outside of government; we believe that various types of conjoint analysis can help elicit this information.

13.7 Using Discrete Choice Methods in Health Care and Education

Contributed by Charles E. Cunningham

Our Patient-Centered Service Research Unit in the Faculty of Health Sciences at McMaster University has worked closely with Dr. Ken Deal of the Marketing Department of the DeGroote School of Business to involve patients in the design of services they receive. The three projects below each began with focus groups and key informant interviews. The themes emerging from these qualitative interviews were used to compose conjoint attributes and levels.

One application involved designing parenting workshops. We began with the design of workshops for parents of children with mental health problems. Parents preferred a scientifically proven program using an active learning process. Their decision to enroll in a parenting skill building program was sensitive to logistical issues such as travel time, workshop schedules, and the availability of child care. Using latent class analysis, we uncovered two strategically important segments with distinct service delivery and advertising preferences. Simulations regarding the redesign of our parenting workshops were consistent with the results of clinical trials and utilization studies, and the validity of our clinic redesign simulations using conjoint data was supported by improvements in subsequent service utilization.

A second application involved improving patient care. The project involved a corporation of five teaching hospitals serving a population of 2.2 million Canadians. We established an annual organizational objective to develop a model of patient-centered care. Focus groups and individual interviews revealed a series of service delivery attributes of special importance to patients. Patients completed partial-profile, discrete choice conjoint surveys in both paper-and-pencil and computer-generated formats. Latent class analysis revealed two segments. Both segments preferred hospitals that ensured patients received more health information and prompt progress reports. Health care teams that worked effectively, an opportunity to learn health promotion skills, and a collaborative approach to service planning were important to a segment of well-educated outpatients. Convenient settings, a welcoming environment, and ease of internal access exerted a greater influence on a segment of inpatient and immigrant families. Simulations predicted that both segments would be willing to trade increased wait times if patients received prompt progress reports, more health information, and the skills to improve their health. The corporation based its model of patient- and family-centered care and its annual quality improvement plan on the results of this conjoint experiment.

A third application involved designing the medical school curriculum. Given the usefulness of conjoint experiments in improving health services, McMaster University decided to use a discrete choice experiment to involve students in the redesign of its small-group, problem-based undergraduate medical education program. Using themes from an electronic decision support lab and key informant interviews, we composed fourteen four-level educational attributes. Medical students completed a Web-administered, partial-profile, discrete choice conjoint experiment. Although increases in enrollment and the high costs associated with small group tutorials led faculty to consider an increase in tutorial group size, student choices revealed a strong preference for smaller groups. Simulations, however, predicted that most students would trade increases in tutorial group size for a more structured, concept-based curriculum integrating tutorial group, clinical skills, and clerkship activities. Through market simulations, we predicted an additional increase in preference if the savings associated with increases in tutorial group size were reinvested in new e-learning technologies. In the fall of 2004, McMaster University introduced the new Compass Curriculum—an approach to medical education consistent with the results of this conjoint experiment.

13.8 Analysis of Women's Preferences for Place of Child Delivery in Rural Tanzania

Contributed by Margaret E. Kruk and Peter Rockers

Ninety-nine percent of the world's 500,000 maternal deaths each year occur in developing countries, and there is a consensus in the international community that delivery in health facilities could greatly reduce that figure. Unfortunately, only one-third of women in rural Tanzania deliver in health facilities, despite widespread geographical availability of health facilities and despite use of health clinics for prenatal care and other conditions. Patient preferences and expectations of the clinic clearly differ for different health needs. Does supply of drugs matter more than distance? Are either of these more important than the provider's attitude? Understanding women's preferences for clinical services for childbirth may help policymakers prioritize where to spend scarce health dollars. The final aim is increasing use of the health system for delivery and, hopefully, reducing maternal deaths.

We used conjoint analysis methods to estimate the relative worth of different features of health facilities to women from rural Tanzania in considering where to deliver their next child. Women were asked to select a facility for their next delivery based on six attributes: distance, cost, type of provider, attitude of provider, availability of drugs and equipment, and free transport. The two most important facility attributes for women were a respectful provider attitude (provider who smiles and listens carefully) and availability of drugs and medical equipment. Results from the conjoint analysis were consistent with women's past choice of delivery facility, suggesting congruence with revealed preference.

In order to assess the extent to which focused investments and policy reforms in the Tanzanian health system would increase utilization of primary care facilities, we conducted simulations reflecting potential changes to facilities, and we calculated projected shares of preference for these facilities versus delivering at home among women. These policy simulations suggested that, if provider performance could be improved and drugs and medical equipment were reliably present, a large majority of women would choose to deliver in health facilities. Our results provide a preliminary road map for policymakers to begin tackling health system reforms to reduce the high rates of maternal mortality in their populations. Real-life experiments that address the key factors identified by women could be used to test the real-world impact on facility delivery rates.

In sum, if health system reforms in developing countries are to be successful, they must account for patient preferences or else risk underutilization with disastrous health effects. One glaring example of this can be seen in the high rate of maternal mortality and low levels of facility delivery in rural Tanzania. Conjoint analysis is a feasible and informative method for eliciting population preferences for health system reforms in developing countries.

13.9   How Conjoint Analysis Is Used at Microsoft

Contributed by Christopher N. Chapman

"We're pricing this product at $99. But is that the best price? What if we charged $10 more or $20 less? Is the product attractive enough to make up more than the price difference?" At Microsoft Hardware, where we make retail consumer PC accessories such as mice and keyboards, these questions were common several years ago. Our products fit into existing retail price bands alongside competitors, but the match between a product idea and a specific price band was sometimes difficult to establish.

Besides looking at price points and product fit, we had many other questions related to portfolio management. If we needed to fill a specific retail price point, which product and set of features would do best? How should we select features at one price point so as not to adversely impact products at other prices? Among several possible products or features we could develop, which would appeal most to customers?

A turning point came when we posed these questions to Dr. Edwin Love of the University of Washington School of Business (now at Western Washington University), an expert on innovation strategy. We asked him if there were methods that would help us. "Sure," he said. "Its a straightforward application of choice-based conjoint analysis." He visited Microsoft Hardware to present the research foundations and a plan for our product teams. Then, as a pilot project, we funded a series of studies in one of our hardware product lines.

Conjoint analysis is often applied late in a product cycle to establish pricing and estimate demand shortly before product release. We felt this was sub-optimal, that it would be better to learn about price, demand, and feature preference at the earliest possible time, the point at which a product concept is selected and before formal development is launched. Accordingly, our first conjoint research projects looked at innovative products and focused on gauging customer interest among multiple potential products. By understanding customer prioritization early, we could better decide which products should move into formal development. For a given product concept, we were also able to prioritize the features for the engineering teams. After initial successes, we began to use conjoint methods broadly across an entire product line.

For this kind of product selection research, we commonly use choice-based conjoint analysis paired with qualitative focus groups. Because innovative product concepts are confidential, we cannot include them in traditional online surveys (which are easy to capture and leak), yet we need more rigorous data than focus group discussions can provide. Also, we often need to demonstrate product concepts in depth to ensure that respondents understand them. Our solution is to recruit focus groups from the target market, show them product concepts, and then administer a conjoint survey within the focus group setting. To avoid bias, we survey respondents before they have had a chance to discuss concepts and influence one another. We follow the conjoint survey with open group discussion as with traditional focus groups, and we use that discussion to drill down on specific aspects of the conjoint results.

This combination of quantitative and qualitative research yields rich and detailed information. It preserves confidentiality with nondisclosure agreements and control of product visuals and descriptions, yet obtains rigorous market estimates of product preference and individual-level results for respondents. Because the survey typically takes only fifteen to twenty minutes of focus group time, we are able to supplement the quantitative data with rich respondent discussion, learning not only what they prefer, but also why. This gives product teams rigorous data for strategic selection and forecasting, along with more in-depth understanding of consumer attitudes and preferences. This process addresses concerns about the reliability of focus group data while providing the opportunity for product teams to experience the power of direct consumer feedback.

How well does it work? This is an ongoing question that we are beginning to answer rigorously. We examine the reliability of conjoint data in three ways: correlating conjoint focus group data to results from other studies and traditional online conjoint surveys, looking at the correspondence of conjoint forecasts to real market data, and tracking the internal influence and adoption of conjoint analysis across largely independent product teams.

In terms of focus group conjoint reliability, we have conducted two comparisons and found excellent correspondence. Our first study looked at the agreement between focus groups, examining the ranking of new product concepts in groups of 40 and 49 respondents. We found rank-order agreement on the two most appealing product concepts. Among the top six product concepts in each group, there was inclusion agreement on five concepts—the same five concepts were among the top six in both groups. Our second study examined product preference between focus group data and online survey data. An in-person conjoint exercise with 79 focus group respondents estimated a new product's customer preference at 37 to 51 percent (80% confidence interval range), while a corresponding online survey across the United States with 595 respondents estimated preference at 41 to 46 percent. The focus group estimate had a large spread because of the small sample size, but it was centered very closely around the larger-sample estimate. The average in both surveys was 44 percent.

We tolerate large confidence intervals obtained from focus group data in order to gain the advantages of deeper understanding, cost reduction, and faster turnaround. When we need tighter estimates for demand forecasting, we use larger-sample, online studies. The key to success with smaller samples is to recruit representative samples from the test markets (testing in Redmond, Washington, for example, would not be appropriate in our case) and to have enough sample to achieve stable results. We typically test eight to ten groups of ten people each for each country of interest.

We are beginning to examine the validity of conjoint results versus actual market data by administering conjoint surveys periodically with online respondent panels. One conjoint analysis simulation with 1,008 respondents estimated a particular product's preference versus other products at 36 to 40 percent (80% confidence interval), while the most recent retail sales data reported a 38 percent share. Such close correspondence is reassuring and builds confidence in the research. But it is crucial to note that these results are fortuitous. As Bryan Orme discusses in the main text, real market results are influenced by many factors that cannot be simulated in a conjoint survey, such as the effects of advertising, channel distribution, retailer assortment, shelf space, and so forth. Thus, although we appreciate finding close research and market correspondence, we interpret conjoint results as being about consumer preference, assuming all other factors are equal. Conjoint results are not expected to deliver exact market forecasts.

In terms of product team influence, we have seen strong appreciation of the work we are doing. The methods described above have been adopted as standard practice across multiple product lines and have received attention and adoption in other parts of the company. Our work was recently recognized with a divisional award for excellence in research. Along the way, we have developed several extensions of basic conjoint methodology: application across the product lifecycle, deep integration with engineering and development work, application to customer segmentation and early needs identification, and a combination of conjoint methodology with decision modeling to examine potential strategic implications of product decisions and the likely competitive responses. For details, see Chapman, Love, and Alford (2008) and Love and Chapman (2007).

In summary, conjoint analysis and related methods have been increasingly valuable for our market and customer research. Although every new method creates new questions, we have advanced the impact of research on business strategy. With these research methods, processes, and innovations, we obtain better customer and market information earlier in the development cycle, answer more questions for product and management stakeholders, inform strategic trade-offs more directly, and (we believe) learn how to make better, more desirable products for our customers.

Appendix A

Glossary

a priori A Latin term meaning "prior to" or "before the fact." In conjoint analysis, we often say that some attributes have preferences with a priori order. For example, we may know that rational respondents would generally view lower prices to be better than higher prices, higher speeds to be more preferred to lower speeds, etc. In Adaptive Conjoint Analysis (ACA), the researcher can specify that certain attributes have a priori ordering (the levels are ordered from worst to best, or best to worst in terms of preference). This allows ACA to avoid asking respondents to rank or rate the levels explicitly within this attribute, and also influences or constrains the estimated part-worth utilities to follow rational expectations.

ACA See Adaptive Conjoint Analysis.

ACBC See adaptive choice-based conjoint.

adaptive choice-based conjoint Also called ACBC. A computer-administered choice-based conjoint interview proposed by Sawtooth Software that involves three major phases: (1) configurator phase in which respondents specify the product they would most likely purchase by selecting preferred levels for each attribute, (2) screening phase during which respondents are asked whether they would consider as "a possibility" or "not a possibility" each of usually two-dozen or more product concepts constructed based on small variations to the configured product from the previous phase, and (3) choice tasks phase in which respondents choose among the products marked as "a possibility" from the previous phase (usually in sets of three) until an overall winning product is identified. The interview exploits the theory that respondents make purchases by first forming consideration sets (often using non-compensatory heuristics), then by making choices within their consideration sets following compensatory rules. ACBC interviews contain much more information than standard CBC for estimating part-worth utilities. Estimation may be done using conventional hierarchical Bayes (HB) approaches or purely individual-level estimation routines.

The ACBC technique is new, so it is difficult to project the long-term impact on conjoint practice. It seems to offer a promising solution, especially for high-involvement product categories involving about five or more attributes. Preliminary evidence suggests that the ACBC interview is more focused, engaging, and realistic to respondents than standard CBC interview. Respondents are willing to spend double or triple the time over nonadaptive CBC questionnaires with equal or better reported satisfaction with the survey-taking experience. Early results also suggest that the data are superior in terms of predictive accuracy (Johnson and Orme 2007).

Adaptive Conjoint Analysis Also called ACA. A computerized conjoint analysis approach developed by Rich Johnson (1987b), first released as a commercial software package in 1985. Adaptive Conjoint Analysis first asks respondents self-explicated prior information (respondents give level rankings/ratings and attribute importance scores) and then uses that preliminary information to construct customized conjoint questions that are relevant (primarily focus on the attributes of most importance to the respondent) and elicit challenging trade-off decisions. After the respondent answers each question, the system updates its estimate of each respondent's part-worth utilities and finishes the interview after a predetermined number of conjoint questions has been asked.

ACA lets respondents evaluate more attributes and levels without overwhelming or fatiguing the respondent than the traditional conjoint analysis method (full-profile card-sort conjoint). ACA is considered a good technique for product design research, but sometimes is a poor tool for pricing research.

ACA became the most widely used conjoint analysis method and software system in the world. It held this position until about 2000, when choice-based conjoint (CBC) became more widely used as a technique. For related topics, see card-sort conjoint, choice-based conjoint, conjoint analysis, and self-explicated approach.

additivity A fundamental assumption made by most conjoint analysis techniques that the total value of a product is simply equal to the sum of the values of its separate parts (the sum of the part-worth utilities across its relevant attribute levels). The theory of additivity suggests that respondents apply a compensatory rule when considering which product to buy/choose, wherein bad characteristics can be overcome by the presence of other very good characteristics (since the value of good characteristics can compensate for bad characteristics). This simple view of buyer behavior is certainly flawed, but the simplification permits us to build generally useful models of consumer behavior that involve many attributes and levels, using a manageable number of questions asked of each respondent.

In truth, many respondents apply noncompensatory rules, such as rejecting any product that has a particular unacceptable color or brand, or that exceeds a certain price, irrespective of how many other excellent qualities it has. Another example of a noncompensatory rule is when respondents choose any product that reflects their favorite brand label, irrespective of how many other bad characteristics it may have.

Even though the additive rule seems simplistic and restrictive, it actually is flexible enough to represent basic (yet common) manifestations of noncompensatory behavior. For example, if a respondent has *must-avoid* levels and if large enough negative utility weights are given to these levels, then no combination of good product characteristics added together can compensate for a *must-avoid* level under the additive rule.

Researchers have recently compared sophisticated noncompensatory model specifications to models that assume additivity, and have found only minor differences in model performance, even though many respondents in the data set are confirmed to be using noncompensatory rules (Hauser, Ding, and Gaskin 2009).

aggregate model   Also known as pooled analysis.   Models that estimate average part-worth utilities or betas for a group of individuals, rather than for each respondent individually. Aggregate models are often used when there just isn't enough information available within each individual to estimate separate (disaggregate) models for each. Multinomial logit is commonly used as an aggregate model for conjoint/choice analysis. That is not to say, however, that multinomial logit cannot be used to fit group-level or respondent-level models. If there is enough information available within each individual, or if respondent characteristics are crossed by attributes, then multinomial logit can model respondent differences.

allocation-based response   Describes the process wherein respondents distribute a certain number of points across multiple product concepts within a set (choice task). The allocated points typically must add up to a constant sum, such as 10 or 100. Allocation is sometimes used in choice-based conjoint studies when respondents can imagine multiple purchases (such as breakfast cereals that might be purchased over the next ten shopping trips) or the probabilities of prescribing drugs to a pool of patients. Allocation is sometimes referred to as chip allocation because respondents are sometimes given poker chips to move to different product alternatives to demonstrate relative preference. While allocation-based responses, in theory, provide more information for estimating preferences than discrete choices, the process takes much longer than making a simple choice. Also, the requirement that the distributed points must add up to a particular sum may get in the way of respondents expressing their true preferences.

Pinnell (1999) has argued that allocation-based responses are less accurate and useful than well-designed first-choice tasks that consider different purchase occasions. Pinnell has suggested that rather than using allocation in CBC tasks, researchers can first ask respondents what occasions lead to different choices, and then ask respondents to make choices based on different (and customized) occasion scenarios. For example, with beer purchases, people consume different brands depending on the consumption occasion (at home alone or at a party with friends). With breakfast cereal purchases, the choice depends on the individual in the family who will eat the cereal. And, the prescription of medications by doctors depends on the characteristics of the patient. In all three examples, separate models could be built based on the specific occasions, with the results weighted across models to predict overall shares of choice.

alternative See concept.

alternative-specific attribute An attribute (product feature) that only is applicable to a specific alternative in a discrete choice experiment. For example, the attribute *parking fee* is only applicable to the alternative *car* when considering methods of getting to work. Parking fee would not apply to riding the bus or walking. See also alternative-specific design.

alternative-specific constant Also known as ASC. In discrete choice or choice-based conjoint models, each product concept (alternative) typically is associated with, say, a different brand. In addition to the brands, other attributes, such as colors, speeds, and prices, may be included in the choice task. The alternative-specific constant is the remaining utility associated with a product alternative after accounting for all other attributes except the concept label, or in this case, the brand. In this context, it is therefore the brand intercept, or utility for brand. Of course, alternative-specific constants may reflect things other than brand. Transportation options (e.g., bus, car, train, bike) are another common example.

alternative-specific design A more generalized and flexible type of CBC experiment in which competing alternatives (such as methods of getting to work or different types of machines) could involve wholly unique attributes. For example, consider a choice task in which respondents are presented with multiple ways to get to work in a large city: by bus, by car, on a bike, or walking. The attributes that describe the alternative of bus travel (e.g., cost of round trip, frequency of arrival) are entirely different from those for car (e.g., cost of fuel, parking fees). Other alternatives, such as walking or biking, may involve no additional attribute descriptions at all, but indicate constant alternatives. Alternative-specific designs can include both alternative-specific (unique) attributes and common attributes (shared across the alternatives). Some researchers distinguish the general class of flexible discrete choice methods (often referred to as discrete choice modeling, or DCM) that can accommodate alternative-specific attributes from the less-flexible choice-based conjoint approach in which all alternatives share common attributes. The first versions of Sawtooth Software's CBC system could not accommodate alternative-specific designs. The Advanced Design Module for CBC later added some alternative-specific design capabilities.

ASC See alternative-specific constant.

attribute A fundamental product or service characteristic such as brand, color, price, speed, etc. Some refer to attributes as factors or features. Each attribute in conjoint analysis must have at least two levels. For example, the attribute color may be described using levels such as red, green, and blue. Most attributes used in conjoint analysis involve relatively definite (concrete) dimensions. Each attribute should be as unique in meaning and independent from the others as possible. While conjoint analysts cannot include all attributes that influence preference for buying a product or service, often most of the decision process for buyers can be modeled using a reasonably small number of attributes.

availability effect The utility loss or gain for product alternatives when competing alternatives are available within the same choice task. For example, Coke may be negatively affected when Pepsi also is available within the same choice task. In discrete choice (CBC) modeling, researchers using aggregate logit might model availability effects to deal with the limitations of the IIA property. Availability terms are often useful for improving model fit for aggregate logit, but with latent class and HB methods, availability effects are typically not used. Availability effects are an example of cross effects. Including availability effects within a model often adds a great number of terms (parameters to be estimated). Models that include all availability and cross effects are sometimes called "mother logit" models.

balance See level balance, positional balance.

base case scenario Generally refers to the existing or future market situation: the client's product formulations versus the relevant competitors' product formulations. Researchers use the base case scenario to estimate base shares of preference using a market simulator. Then, modifications to the client's products are specified and the market simulation rerun, to see how these changes affect the shares of preference. These are often expressed as changes relative to base case. It is usually advisable to ask clients to specify the base case scenario during the first stages of designing a conjoint analysis study and developing the attribute list. See market simulator and sensitivity analysis for more information.

best/worst conjoint A technique for measuring multiattribute preferences that has similarities to (but is really not a true form of) conjoint analysis. Respondents are shown products described by multiple attributes (each at a prescribed level). But rather than considering the preference for the product as a whole, respondents are asked to indicate which of its attribute levels are its best and worst aspects. For example, in evaluating a PC, a respondent might indicate that the best aspect is its price (e.g., $500), but the worst aspect is the monitor size (e.g., seventeen inches).

Best/worst conjoint is not a true conjoint method because respondents never express their preference for conjoined attributes either as a partial or full concept. The argued benefit of best/worst conjoint analysis is that one can derive utility scores for the levels on a common scale (so that the preference for levels can be directly compared across attributes), whereas no such comparisons can be made with standard conjoint analysis.

Some researchers have used best/worst utility scores for market simulations, which is a questionable practice. Since profiles are never evaluated as a whole, the idea of summing the best/worst utility values across the attribute levels to project market choice for product concepts is flawed. Most informed advocates of best/worst conjoint recognize these flaws, but value the technique for identifying specific levels that may be leveraged in promotional efforts, or which levels are especially detrimental to acceptance of a product. The methods of best/worst conjoint should not be confused with best/worst scaling (also known as MaxDiff), which uses the same modeling approach to deal with the more general problem of scaling multiple items in terms of importance or preference. See maximum difference scaling.

binary attribute A categorical attribute with exactly two levels, such as a yes/no item on a consumer survey or a true/false checklist item. Many product attributes in conjoint studies have exactly two levels. Consider automobile features: sunroof versus no sunroof and extended warranty versus no extended warranty. See categorical attribute.

blocking When there are many more conjoint questions in the total design than any one respondent can evaluate, the questions can be divided into carefully constructed blocks, or subsets of the total design plan. For example, consider a conjoint study with 100 unique conjoint questions. The researcher, realizing that any one respondent does not have the time or ability to evaluate all 100 questions, might divide the questions into five blocks of twenty questions. Each respondent is randomly assigned to receive one of the five blocks (sometimes called questionnaire versions). Ideally, each block of conjoint questions reflects a high degree of level balance (each attribute level occurs nearly an equal number of times). Blocking is often used when the method of interviewing favors managing only a limited number of questionnaire versions (such as with a paper-and-pencil format) and the estimation method involves some type of aggregation or data sharing across respondents. With computerized conjoint methods, it is often useful to give each individual a unique set of carefully constructed conjoint questions. See fixed design.

Bradley-Terry-Luce model Also known as the BTL model. A market simulation model for converting overall utility scores for competing product alternatives to probabilities of choice. Consider utilities for product alternatives a, b, and c for a single individual. Call these utilities U_a, U_b, and U_c. The BTL model states that the probability that this individual will choose product alternative a from the competitive set $\{a, b, c\}$ is

$$P_a = \frac{U_a}{(U_a + U_b + U_c)}$$

For example, if the utilities for alternatives a, b, and c for an individual are $U_a = 30$, $U_b = 40$, and $U_c = 10$, then the probability of this individual choosing product a is

$$P_a = \frac{30}{(30 + 40 + 10)} = 37.5\%$$

while the probabilities of choosing alternatives b and c are

$$P_b = \frac{40}{(30 + 40 + 10)} = 50.0\%$$

$$P_c = \frac{10}{(30 + 40 + 10)} = 12.5\%$$

The shares add to 100 percent. The BTL model requires that the utilities for products be positive values, and that these values be proportional to choice probabilities. The scale (steepness or flatness of shares) for BTL models can be adjusted using the alpha rule, where alpha is a positive value applied as an exponent to the product utilities.

bridging Refers to an approach often used with, but not limited to, card-sort conjoint for dealing with situations in which there are many more attributes than respondents can comfortably evaluate at one time in full profile. For example, consider a study involving eleven attributes. As a simple example of bridging, half of the respondents might be given a questionnaire involving attributes 1 through 6, with the other half receiving a questionnaire involving attributes 6 through 11. Attribute 6 is the common bridge between the two groups of respondents, and permits the results from attributes 1 to 5 to be placed on a commensurate scale with attributes 7 through 11. Bridging designs across respondents necessarily involves data imputation, matching, or pooling results across respondents (aggregation), and the accompanying assumptions of population homogeneity. Bridging is not commonly used today because of these drawbacks.

BTL model See Bradley-Terry-Luce model.

build-your-own (BYO) task See configurator task.

calibration concept Usually refers to the optional final section in Adaptive Conjoint Analysis (ACA) surveys wherein the respondent rates about four to six product concepts each on a 100-point purchase likelihood scale. Each product concept is described using just the most important attributes for that individual. First, the worst possible product concept is shown, followed by the absolute best, with the remaining product concepts falling somewhere in between. The answers are used for scaling the final part-worth utilities for use in the market simulator, especially for purchase likelihood simulations.

The calibration concepts are also used for estimating the reliability of the respondent's answers across the multiple sections of the ACA interview. The resulting reliability score is called the correlation. There is some question regarding the value of calibration concepts and the usefulness of the resulting reliability score.

calibration task Usually refers to the conjoint questions used for estimating part-worth utilities, as opposed to those used for holdout or internal validation purposes.

card-sort conjoint The traditional conjoint analysis approach developed in the early 1970s. Conjoint interviews at that time were done almost exclusively using paper-and-pencil instruments. To facilitate the comparison of often sixteen or more product concepts, each was printed on a separate card. Respondents were instructed to sort (rank) the product concept cards in order from most to least desirable.

Later, when it was discovered that using rating scales provided just as good or slightly better data than ranking, researchers still found it useful to print cards and ask respondents to complete a modified sorting exercise. For example, respondents might be asked to first divide the cards into a few piles, representing those they most liked, least liked, and then those in between. This would establish a good frame of reference and simplify the subsequent step of assigning a preference score (often on a 10- or 100-point scale) to each card, starting from those in the least desirable pile and working toward those in the most desirable pile. Ratings-based rather than ranking-based conjoint soon became more popular, but the term "card-sort conjoint" persisted, sometimes even being applied to studies in which respondents only directly rated the cards or studies in which the product concepts were not printed on cards at all.

CAPI See computer-assisted personal interviewing.

categorical attribute Also known as polytomous attribute, or nominal attribute. Attributes like brand, style, or color, in which the levels represent discrete categories, often with no logical or a priori preference order. Also see binary attribute.

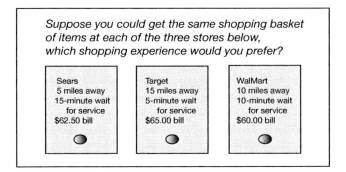

Exhibit A.1. Choice among shopping experiences

CATI See computer-aided telephone interviewing.

CBC Stands for choice-based conjoint. CBC is also the name of a software system for conducting choice-based conjoint, which was first released by Sawtooth Software in 1993. See choice-based conjoint.

chip allocation See allocation-based response.

choice-based conjoint A relatively recent flavor of conjoint analysis and the most popular current conjoint-based technique (as of about 2000). Choice-based conjoint (CBC) goes by many names, including discrete choice modeling (DCM), discrete choice, or choice analysis. What distinguishes CBC from earlier conjoint methods is that respondents are shown a few (often three to five) product or service concepts at a time and are asked which one they would choose. Consider the example of shopping experiences in exhibit A.1.

Each question in CBC is usually called a choice task. On a CBC questionnaire, typically around a dozen or more choice tasks are presented to respondents, each one containing a different variation of product concepts.

Researchers have valued CBC because the choice task more closely mimics reality: Respondents choose from a set of available product alternatives, or they defer their purchase. Indeed, buyers do not formally rate different product alternatives in the marketplace and then buy the one that has the highest score. Rather, they simply view the alternatives and make a choice. The argument is that if researchers are interested in projecting market choices, then they are better served by collecting choice data to begin with.

Unfortunately, choice-based conjoint is an inefficient way to collect data. Respondents must read a lot of information (for example, three or four product alternatives described by three to six attributes) before providing an answer. And the answer only indicates which alternative is best, with no indication of strength of preference. No relative information is collected about the rejected products. Moreover, choice data are more difficult to analyze than ratings-based conjoint methods. There is typically not enough information to estimate a full set of preferences for each individual (entirely independent of the others), so some type of aggregation or data sharing has been necessary. Typical analytical methods for estimating preference from CBC include logit, latent class, and hierarchical Bayes (HB) analysis.

choice set See set.

choice simulator See market simulator.

common attribute See generic attribute.

compensatory model See additivity.

composite factor Also known as composite attribute or superattribute. An attribute that reflects the feasible combinations of two or more attributes. Composite factors are useful for dealing with the problems of interactions and/or prohibitions between two or more attributes. For example, consider two attributes, model of car and color:

Model	*Color*
Sedan	Black
Coupe	Red
Limousine	

Red does not make sense with limousine. Furthermore, there may be an interaction effect between color and model. For example, the combination of red with coupe may go particularly well—representing higher utility than might be suggested by the separate main effects of model and color. To overcome both of these problems, a single composite categorical attribute might be constructed that involves the five feasible combinations of the two attributes:

Model with Color
Black sedan
Black coupe
Black limousine
Red sedan
Red coupe

Separate part-worth utilities would be measured for each of these levels.

composition rule A rule hypothesized by the researcher that respondents employ when assigning (composing) the overall preference for a product alternative. The additive rule is the most commonly assumed composition rule.

compositional model Some methods of preference estimation ask respondents to directly indicate the utility scores for attribute levels. Self-explicated scaling is an example of a compositional model. The preferences or utility scores for the many levels of the attributes are directly indicated using rating scales, and the analyst composes the overall utility of a product alternative by adding the utility scores across its levels. Analytical approaches that use respondents' ratings of individual features to predict an overall rating for product concepts (such as with regression analysis) are also termed compositional.

In contrast, conjoint analysis is a decompositional approach, starting with total product evaluations (in terms of preference or choice) and backing out or decomposing part-worth utility weights that explain the observed product evaluations.

computer-assisted personal interviewing Also known as CAPI. Data collection by using a laptop or personal computer to administer a survey.

computer-aided telephone interviewing Also known as CATI. When professional interviewers use computers to conduct telephone surveys.

concept Generally refers to a product offering defined using one level from each of multiple attributes in the study. For example, the array [Honda, 4-door, Red, $20,000] describes a product concept. Synonyms are alternative, profile, stimulus, and treatment.

conditional pricing A specialized kind of choice-based conjoint (CBC) approach in which the price ranges are customized depending on the brand, or another attribute or combination of attributes.

In conditional pricing, the researcher first determines a constant number of price levels to be tested for each, say, brand level. For example, the researcher might specify three levels of price. Then the researcher specifies a custom set of prices (in this case, three) for each brand: Brand A might have prices [$10, $15, $20], and premium Brand B might have prices [$20, $30, $40]. Conditional pricing allows researchers to create more realistic experiments, but the results are a bit more difficult to model and interpret. Furthermore, if the conditional prices do not follow careful guidelines, the model may not fit the data well.

Conditional pricing may be considered a specialized type of alternative-specific design. See also alternative-specific design.

configurator task A choice task in which respondents configure the product they would be most likely to purchase by selecting a preferred level from each of multiple attributes. Most of the attributes involve incremental prices for enhanced levels. A total price is shown that interactively changes as respondents make level selections. The price typically starts at some base amount, given basic/default product features. Respondents modify the product specifications (or retain them at default levels) until they are happy with the final configured product. Because of the interactive nature of the task, it is almost always implemented as a computerized survey.

Configurator tasks are quite reflective of some purchase processes, for example buying a PC on Dell's Website. Part-worth utility estimates can be estimated from configurator tasks (Bakken and Bayer 2001; Liechty, Ramaswamy, and Cohen 2001; Johnson, Orme, and Pinnell 2006; Rice and Bakken 2006), though the utilities can differ significantly from standard CBC tasks (Johnson, Orme, and Pinnell 2006). Clients and respondents alike are drawn to configurator tasks, but the data are sparse compared with data from traditional conjoint tasks. Configurator tasks may require significantly larger sample sizes than traditional conjoint tasks. And pooled analysis is the usually rule for configurator tasks.

conjoint analysis A quantitative market research technique that asks respondents to rank, rate, or choose among multiple products or services, where each product is described using multiple characteristics, called attribute levels. Some think the word *conjoint* comes from the idea that respondents are asked to trade off product characteristics CONsidered JOINTly. While this is a useful mnemonic and an accurate depiction, the word "conjoint" really means joined together or conjoined (think of conjoined twins). What sets conjoint analysis apart from other multiattribute preference measurement methods (such as self-explicated methods) is that respondents consider their preference for whole product concepts each described using more than one attribute level (product characteristics such as brand, color, speed, or price). The researcher carefully manipulates the appearance of attribute levels in the product concepts, such that the unique contributions of each level can be estimated independently. Using statistical methods, analysts deduce what preference scores for the levels could explain the observed product evaluations.

Generally, there are three main flavors of conjoint analysis. The first conjoint analysis approach, full-profile, card-sort conjoint, was introduced to marketers by Green and Rao (1971). Later, Adaptive Conjoint Analysis and choice-based conjoint were introduced. Some people reserve the word conjoint analysis to refer to sorting-based or ratings-based approaches, and do not use the term when referencing choice-based approaches such as CBC (discrete choice modeling). See Adaptive Conjoint Analysis, card-sort conjoint, choice-based conjoint, and full-profile.

conjoint value analysis Traditional full-profile conjoint analysis, sometimes referred to as card-sort conjoint. CVA is an acronym for conjoint value analysis and the name for Sawtooth Software's package for traditional full-profile conjoint analysis. CVA was originally released in 1990 as a system focused on component-based price sensitivity measurement. For example, CVA was designed especially for measuring the price sensitivity for the separate parts of a fast-food meal, such as the hamburger, the fries, and the drink. Later, in 1996, CVA was updated and repositioned as a general full-profile conjoint analysis tool. CVA supports either one-concept-at-a-time or pairwise (two concepts at a time) presentation. It supports either rank-order (sorting) or rating data. CVA is used less often than ACA or especially CBC software, but it has unique advantages for small scope studies (few attributes), especially those involving relatively small sample sizes. See full profile and card-sort conjoint.

conjunctive choice rule A noncompensatory evaluation heuristic in which a respondent establishes cutoff points of acceptability for each of many relevant attributes for a complex product or service. If a product alternative meets the threshold acceptability requirements on all key attributes, it is selected or moved into the consideration set. Otherwise, it is rejected. The conjunctive choice heuristic is one of many simplification strategies that respondents may employ to deal with the challenge of choosing among many complex competitive offerings. Conjoint analysis models usually assume a compensatory (additive) rule, in which negative aspects of a product may be compensated for by other desirable qualities. Additive models, therefore, may have some difficulty fitting the data well if many respondents consistently use noncompensatory choice processes. See additivity, elimination-by-aspects choice rule, lexicographic choice rule, and unacceptables.

connectivity A required property of MaxDiff (maximum difference scaling). Each item in the study should be directly or indirectly compared to every other item in the study. Connectivity allows all items to be placed on a common scale. Connectivity can either be established through direct connections (each item appears with every other item in at least one MaxDiff set) or indirect connections. Indirect connections are those established by leveraging the law of transitivity. For example, if A is compared (and preferred) to B and B is compared (and preferred) to C, we know, in turn, that A is preferred to C.

With MaxDiff studies, it is common for respondents to receive different blocks (versions) of the questionnaire, each containing different combinations of items assembled in sets (tasks or questions). When pooling information across respondents to estimate item scores, it is necessary only that connectivity be established when considering all the information across blocks in the study. Though it is also preferred to have connectivity within each respondent's block.

constant alternative In choice-based conjoint, one of the available options may be a fixed piece of text or graphic, such as the *none* choice (indicating that the respondent would not select any of these product concepts if these were the only ones available). Any of these fixed stimuli may be considered a constant alternative. As an example, consider a choice task describing different ways to get to work. See exhibit A.2.

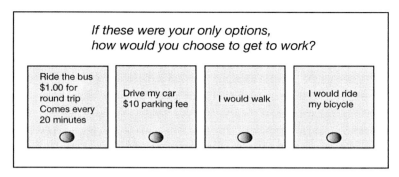

Exhibit A.2. Choice task with constant alternatives

The alternatives for bus and car are not fixed in nature, but include other attributes that vary, such as cost for the round trip on the bus. "I would walk" and "I would ride my bicycle" are constant alternatives, and include no other attributes with varying levels to modify them.

constant sum See allocation-based response.

constrained estimation See constraints.

constraints Also known as monotonicity constraints. Some attributes, such as speed, quality, and cost, often have known a priori order. For example, we know that higher speeds are preferred to lower speeds, higher quality is better than lower quality, and higher costs are worse than lower costs (all else held equal). However, estimated part-worth utilities for individuals (or even for small groups) often violate these rational expectations (display reversals). Reasons for reversals include random error and/or respondent inattention. One possible remedy is to impose utility constraints (often called monotonicity constraints, where monotonicity refers to utilities required to be either uniformly increasing or uniformly decreasing across an attribute range). Through constrained estimation, one might enforce that the utility of higher speed exceeds the utility of lower speed. The researcher must be absolutely certain that all rational respondents would agree with the constraints.

context effect A cue or context within conjoint studies that affects how respondents process information and assign value to or choose among product profiles. Examples include the number and positional order of questions and attributes, how many levels are used per attribute, how many product alternatives are shown, and dominance.

continuous attribute Also known as a quantitative attribute. Attributes that are quantitative in nature, with numerical levels such as amounts of price, weight, or speed, modeled using a linear or curvilinear function. See attribute, ideal point model, and ideal vector model.

convergence A term often used to describe the point at which part-worth utility estimation routines (e.g., multinomial logit, latent class, or hierarchical Bayes) settle in on a stable solution.

The multinomial logit routine starts with initial random estimates of part-worth utilities and successively improves these estimates over a number of steps or iterations. In each step, each part-worth is modified in a direction and at a rate of progress that is expected to improve the fit to the data. Theoretically, this process could continue indefinitely, with the most recent estimate of part-worths only being minutely better than the last, resulting in the best-fit solution measured to a staggering number of decimal places of precision. Analysts typically impose some stopping-point rule, indicating that a certain degree of precision is enough. Once the solution does not improve by an amount greater than this threshold, it is assumed that the process has arrived at, or converged, on the optimal solution.

With multinomial logit, no matter what the starting point, one converges on the maximum likelihood solution (to within any desired number of decimal places of precision). But with latent class analysis (which simultaneously detects underlying segments of relatively homogenous respondents and develops a logit model characterizing preferences within each) the solution obtained upon convergence may be suboptimal, representing a local minima. Starting from a different random starting point may produce a better solution. For this reason, analysts usually try multiple starting points and retain the best solution.

In hierarchical Bayes (HB) analysis, arbitrary starting points are again employed, and usually many thousands of steps or iterations are undertaken to improve those part-worth utility estimates. Over the first hundreds or thousands of iterations, these part-worths, and other measures of fit to the data, trend in a definite direction. The path to convergence with HB is never a smooth, steady path, but more like a random, rambling walk. Once the values randomly oscillate with no perceptible trend, the analyst assumes convergence. If the proper input settings are used, HB eventually converges to a model that provides a true and unbiased estimate of the population's preferences. If proper input settings (especially priors) are not used, HB results may never converge to true part-worth estimates.

correlation A general statistical term referring to whether one variable tends to have a linear relationship with and can explain the variance in another. In ACA, correlation often refers to the consistency score computed for each individual indicating how consistently the responses to the calibration concepts section can be predicted by the earlier responses to the Priors and Pairs sections. The correlation score is sometimes used to discard ACA respondents that have lower consistencies. In that context, one often refers to a correlation cutoff.

counts Refers to a simple method for summarizing respondent preferences in CBC experiments showing the probability of respondents selecting a particular attribute level (such as a brand, color, or price level) given that it was available for choice. Typical counts probabilities may look like this:

Alternative	Probability
$10	0.26
$12	0.21
$14	0.15

These results show that $10 was the most preferred, being chosen 26 percent of the times that it was available within choice tasks. The counts proportions do not necessarily sum to 100 percent but are treated as relative choice probabilities with ratio scaling properties. Counts are often used as a preliminary and fast analysis procedure prior to estimating a model using more advanced procedures. For counts to accurately isolate the effect of the levels for each separate attribute, the questionnaire design must be orthogonal or near-orthogonal.

cross-effects See also availability effects. The effect of a product alternative's features upon another product alternative's choice probability. For example, if Coke is available in a choice task, it might negatively affect Pepsi's probability of being chosen. This cross-effect, caused by the presence or absence of an alternative, is known as an availability effect. As another example, Coke's price can have a strong effect on the probability of choosing Pepsi. Two highly substitutable alternatives, such as Coke and Pepsi, might have strong positive cross-effects.

Cross-effects are sometimes directly modeled with CBC data, whereas ACA and traditional full-profile conjoint do not support the direct modeling of these terms. However, market simulators built on individual-level part-worth models (whether estimated using CBC or another conjoint method) can be used to derive cross-effects by observing how the introduction of one product alternative affects another alternative's share within competitive simulation scenarios.

cross-elasticities The change in alternative A's choice probability due to a change in alternative B's product characteristics. The most common example is the cross-elasticity of price. For example, if Coke raises its price, it should have a strong positive effect on the choice probability for Pepsi. Cross-elasticities are generally positive. For example, a cross-elasticity of 0.50 between Coke and Pepsi means that for every 1 percent increase in the price of Coke, Pepsi experiences a 0.50 percent increase in quantity demanded.

CVA See conjoint value analysis.

DCM See discrete choice modeling.

decompositional model Conjoint analysis is often referred to as a decompositional method of preference estimation, because rather than directly ask respondents to indicate their preferences for attributes and levels, these are statistically deduced (decomposed) from the overall product evaluations of conjoint profiles (cards).

degrees of freedom In traditional full-profile conjoint analysis (such as with Sawtooth Software's CVA system), degrees of freedom usually refers to how many additional observations are available at the individual level beyond the number of parameters to be estimated. The more degrees of freedom, the more information is available at the respondent level to stabilize part-worth utility estimates. For example, if there are 10 parameters (i.e., weights, coefficients, or terms) to be estimated, and each respondent evaluates 18 product concepts, there are $18 - 10 = 8$ degrees of freedom. Generally, degrees of freedom are equal to $(t - K - k + 1)$, where t is the number of conjoint questions per respondent, K is the total number of levels in the study, and k is the total number of attributes. The $+1$ is not included in the equation if no intercept is estimated.

design Sometimes, conjoint analysts refer to a design as the number of attributes in the study and the number of levels per attribute. Thus, one might comment, "We have a pretty complicated design, with seventeen attributes, each with between two and six levels." As one develops the actual conjoint survey questions, the design refers to the combination of attributes and levels that make up the many product concepts. In the traditional form of conjoint analysis, all respondents generally see the same set of conjoint questions. In that case, the design is fixed for all respondents. In Adaptive Conjoint Analysis, the combination of attribute levels (the design) shown in the pairwise conjoint questions is customized for each individual. In computerized choice-based conjoint analysis, each individual typically receives a unique combination of product features across the choice tasks (often referred to as a randomized design). When choice-based conjoint data are analyzed by pooling respondents together, the design reflects the sum total of all attribute level combinations across all concepts, tasks, and respondents. For those that are statistically inclined, the design is described by the dummy- or effects-coded independent variable matrix.

design matrix The often dummy- or effects-coded independent variable matrix that reflects the product combinations shown in the conjoint analysis questionnaire. This is also known as the X matrix. See design.

disaggregate models Generally refers to models developed within individuals separately. Adaptive Conjoint Analysis, traditional full-profile conjoint (CVA), and self-explicated preference modeling are usually analyzed within each individual, meaning that a unique set of part-worth utilities is developed for each. Choice-based conjoint data, in contrast, were historically analyzed by pooling across respondents (aggregate analysis) because there wasn't enough information available within each individual (given the available methods) to stabilize the estimates. Recently, hierarchical Bayes (HB) analysis has permitted disaggregate estimation from choice-based conjoint data. Latent class analysis also provides some degree of disaggregation, even though respondents within each class are assumed to have identical preferences, with random noise.

discrete choice modeling Also known as DCM. This term is commonly applied to choice-based conjoint analysis (CBC), though it actually is a much broader classification and CBC represents a small subset of DCM models. DCM refers to a class of models in which the nominal dependent variable reflects choice. Many DCM models are built to explain scanner sales data using consumer/household characteristics. Some experienced analysts (particularly those with an econometric background) point out that DCM encompasses more flexible kinds of choice experiments than conjoint analysis wherein different product alternatives can have unique (alternative-specific) sets of attributes and choice tasks can include multiple constant alternatives. See alternative-specific designs and constant alternatives.

dollar metrics Some researchers like to convert the part-worth utility differences between attribute levels to dollar amounts, representing the amount respondents would be willing to pay to get an improved level over a less desirable level. This exercise requires that a price attribute be included in the conjoint study and that the researcher have a great deal of confidence that the slope (importance) of price has been accurately estimated. One approach to creating dollar metrics involves converting the part-worths for price levels to dollars per utile, and applying that dollar-based scale to the differences between levels for the other attributes.

This type of analysis is often referred to as willingness to pay or converting part-worths to monetary equivalents. Willingness to pay can also be derived from conducting sensitivity analysis using market simulators. Many consider the market simulation approach to be a more accurate method for converting differences in preference between levels to dollar metrics.

Dollar metrics can also refer to a case in which respondents evaluate a product profile in terms of the dollar amount they would be willing to pay (or would expect to pay) for that alternative (rather than the typical rating or ranking). Or, with a pairwise comparison approach, respondents may express how much more they are willing to pay for one product alternative over the other.

dominance When a product alternative or conjoint card is clearly superior in utility to competing alternatives, this is termed dominance. A high degree of dominance within a conjoint or discrete choice questionnaire usually is not desirable. A choice of a dominant alternative is less informative for refining respondent preferences than a more thoughtful trade-off among alternatives wherein there isn't an obvious choice. See also utility balance.

double-counting Overweighting of attributes that have overlap in meaning, most evident in partial-profile, ACA, and especially self-explicated scaling. Consider two attributes that refer to essentially the same thing (e.g., horsepower and acceleration). If respondents assess the importance of each attribute separately (as in self-explicated scaling), the resulting scores added across attributes would overstate the true overall effect of engine power. Double-counting distorts the assessment of attribute importances and reduces the accuracy of market simulations.

With partial-profile exercises, when overlapping attributes are not shown together in product concepts, each has an opportunity to capture the effect of engine power. In full-profile exercises, most respondents recognize that the two attributes essentially refer to the same dimension, and double-counting is reduced. Problems from double-counting are avoided when attributes are formulated as independent in meaning.

The importance of price relative to other attributes can be biased downward due to double-counting of the nonprice attributes. Price, it is argued, comprises a unique utility dimension, and is therefore not often double-counted. When other attributes are double-counted and price is single-counted, the relative importance of price is inappropriately decreased. This is often seen in ACA projects that include both self-explicated and partial-profile conjoint elements, especially in ACA projects with ten or more attributes.

dual conjoint Dual conjoint refers to the combination of Adaptive Conjoint Analysis (ACA) and a second conjoint technique such as choice-based conjoint (CBC) or traditional full-profile conjoint within the same questionnaire. The second half of the survey (the traditional conjoint or CBC part) is often referred to as the "dual," and usually includes brand, price, and a few other key attributes. The reason additional conjoint questions are included after ACA is to provide more accurate price sensitivity measurement than is available through ACA. The ACA weight (importance) for price is often adjusted to incorporate the information from the dual.

dual-response *none* A strategy for eliciting the *none* response in a choice-based conjoint questionnaire using a second-stage question after each choice task. For example, rather than ask respondents to indicate which they would choose among the four alternatives a, b, c, and "none of the above," respondents are first asked to choose among three alternatives a, b, or c, and are next asked whether they would actually purchase the product alternative chosen in the first stage. Respondents provide a yes/no or buy/no buy response in the second stage. See *none* concept.

dummy coding A data coding method for representing the presence or absence of product features, in which a 0 means "not present" and a 1 means "present." Dummy coding is used when specifying the independent variables (the design matrix) in an ordinary least-squares regression model, such as Sawtooth Software's CVA program for full-profile conjoint analysis. Dummy coding is done behind the scenes during part-worth utility estimation under the CVA system, so it is hidden and automatic to the user. Many researchers use dummy coding to represent categorical factors (such as conjoint attributes) in building their own predictive models.

We represent a k-leveled attribute using $(k - 1)$ independent variables to avoid linear dependency (the situation in which one column of the design matrix can be perfectly predicted by a linear combination of other independent variables). For example, for a two-level attribute such as Color: Red or $Blue$, $(k - 1)$, or one dummy-coded variable (as a single column in the design matrix) is specified. We select one of the levels to be a "reference" level, meaning that the dummy-coded value (and the resulting part-worth utility) is zero. In this example, we will specify Red as the reference (zero) level. The dummy-coded independent variable to indicate color is

Attribute Level	Code
Red	0
Blue	1

Let us assume that color now has three levels: Red, $Blue$, and $Green$. In the case of three-level attributes, the attribute is coded as $(k - 1)$ or two columns. Again, one level is arbitrarily chosen as the reference (zero) level. If we select Red as the reference level, the dummy-coded independent variables to indicate color at three levels are

Attribute Level	First Code	Second Code
Red	0	0
Blue	1	0
Green	0	1

The estimated beta (part-worth utility weight) for the first independent variable (first column) applies to $Blue$, and the second column to $Green$. These two part-worth utilities are scaled with respect to Red being set at zero, and represent the gain (or loss) for each color compared to the reference color of Red. The part-worth utility weight for Red is zero.

effect A dimension of preference that the researcher seeks to capture using a parameter in a conjoint analysis or choice model. For example, a main effect reflects the independent utility of each attribute, holding all other attributes constant. An interaction effect reflects the utility when multiple attributes combine. The precision with which the estimated parameters capture these underlying effects is given by the standard errors of the estimates.

effects coding A data coding method for representing the levels of categorical attributes. In Sawtooth Software's CBC programs, effects coding is used when specifying the independent variables (the design matrix). Effects coding is done behind the scenes during part-worth utility estimation, so it is hidden and automatic to the user. We represent a k-leveled attribute using $(k-1)$ independent variables to avoid linear dependency (the situation in which one column of the design matrix can be perfectly predicted by a linear combination of other independent variables). For example, for a two-level attribute such as color (*Red* or *Blue*), $(k-1)$ or one effects-coded variable (as a single column in the design matrix) is specified. We select one of the levels to be a reference level, and specify -1 for all columns associated with that attribute. If we specify *Red* as the reference level, the effects-coded independent variable to indicate color is

Attribute Level	Code
Red	-1
Blue	1

For color at three levels (*Red*, *Blue*, and *Green*), the attribute is coded as $(k-1)$ or two columns. If we select *Red* as the reference level, the effects-coded independent variables to indicate color at three levels are

Attribute Level	First Code	Second Code
Red	-1	-1
Blue	1	0
Green	0	1

Effects coding is very similar to dummy coding, except that the utility weight of the reference level is set to negative the sum of the other levels within the same attribute, rather than being held at zero. So, if the part-worth utilities for *Blue* and *Green* are -1 and -0.5, respectively, *Red* is negative their sum, or +1.5. With effects coding, the part-worths are zero-centered within each attribute, and if interaction terms are estimated, the main effects and interaction terms may be interpreted independently.

efficiency Relates to how precisely a given set of conjoint questions can estimate the parameters of interest. Efficiency is expressed relative to some ideal or to another set of conjoint questions (design) under consideration. For example, consider two conjoint questionnaires, A and B, with the same number of conjoint questions covering the same attributes and levels (but showing different combinations of product concepts). If the overall design efficiency of A is twice as efficient as design B, you can obtain the same degree of precision for part-worth utility estimates (assuming pooled estimation) with half as many respondents under questionnaire A compared to questionnaire B.

Sometimes efficiency is expressed as a percentage from 0 to 100 percent, reflecting the efficiency of this particular set of questions (design) relative to an ideal design (holding the number of conjoint questions constant). Efficiency is not the only criterion that should be considered when developing a conjoint survey. Aside from design efficiency, researchers should ensure that enough conjoint questions are asked of respondents to obtain stable estimation and that enough respondents are included in the sample.

elimination-by-aspects choice rule A noncompensatory evaluation heuristic in which a respondent sequentially discards available product alternatives that do not meet certain cutoff points until one winner is remaining. Starting with the attribute of most importance and working to the attribute of least importance, product alternatives that do not meet a certain threshold of acceptability are eliminated until only one remains. The elimination-by-aspects choice heuristic is one of many kinds of simplification strategies that respondents may employ to deal with the challenge of choosing among many complex competitive offerings. Conjoint analysis models usually assume a compensatory (additive) rule, where negative aspects of a product may be compensated for by other desirable qualities. Additive models therefore may have some difficulty fitting the data well if many respondents consistently use noncompensatory choice processes. See also additivity, conjunctive choice rule, lexicographic choice rule, and unacceptables.

environmental correlation Also known as interattribute correlation. When the levels of two attributes naturally correlate in real-world products. Examples include horsepower, maximum speed, and fuel efficiency.

exponent See scale factor.

external effects The results from conjoint market simulators sometimes do not match actual market shares very well. Perhaps the researcher made a fundamental error such as not including the right attributes/levels or not interviewing the right people. However, many times the lack of fit to real-world shares is due to other factors in the real-world marketplace that the conjoint analysis interview and resulting model does not consider.

External effects are factors outside the conjoint analysis model that shape real market shares, including distribution, awareness, effectiveness of sales force, out-of-stock conditions, and time on the market. Some researchers like to factor these influences back into the simulator by specifying external effect factors—multiplicative adjustments (fudge factors or shifts in a brand intercept) that adjust a product's share of preference up or down.

In general, most researchers avoid using external effect adjustments, preferring not to alter the fundamental share of a product in market simulation results. Adjusting the shares using external effect factors changes the sensitivities of the attributes for the altered product, such as its price elasticity. An exception to this is multi-store simulators, which can correct for differences in product distribution without changing the price sensitivities of the products.

external validity The ability of a conjoint analysis model or market simulator to accurately predict some outcome outside of the realm of the survey, such as a subsequent choice or purchase by an individual, or market shares for a population. External validity is the most demanding standard of predictive performance.

factor See attribute.

factorial design See fractional factorial for discussion.

finite mixture models See latent class analysis.

first-choice model Also known as maximum utility rule. After conjoint data have been collected and part-worth utilities have been estimated for the sample, researchers often conduct market simulations. Researchers consider different product concepts that may be available for choice by respondents in a hypothetical competitive market scenario. A first-choice model assumes respondents buy or choose the product alternative from the competitive set that has the highest total utility, as determined by summing the part-worth utilities associated with the levels describing each product. The percent of respondents projected to choose each alternative in the competitive scenario is summarized, and the results are referred to as shares of first choice. For example, in the competitive set $\{A, B, C\}$, product A may be preferred by 40 percent of the sample, product B by 50 percent, and product C by 10 percent.

The first-choice model is the most intuitive market simulation model to understand, it is easy to compute, and the resulting shares of choice are invariant to the scaling of the underlying part-worths. The first-choice model requires individual-level part-worth utilities. It is the least susceptible (of all market simulation rules) to IIA problems. That is, it deals better with substitution effects among very similar competitors. But the first-choice model is often too extreme, assuming that respondents will choose with certainty the product alternative that has the highest share, irrespective of whether the selected product is very much or only slightly better than the other alternatives in the market scenario.

first-order effect An interaction effect that occurs when two attributes combine. An interaction effect between three attributes is called a second-order effect, etc. For more detail, see interaction effect.

fixed design Sometimes researchers choose to employ just a single version of a choice-based conjoint questionnaire, having determined that distributing many unique questionnaire versions (each containing different product concept formulations) across respondents is not necessary to obtain a reasonable estimation of the effects (part-worth utilities) of interest. For example, with limited attributes and levels per attribute, and especially when interactions are not of concern, a fixed series of choice tasks may be quite adequate to obtain good precision of part-worth estimates. Even though there may be just one set of, say, eighteen choice tasks, it is wise to rotate the order of presentation to respondents to reduce order, learning, and context effects. With traditional, full-profile conjoint, the typical approach is to use a single fixed design plan. See blocking.

fixed task Often refers to a choice-based conjoint (CBC) task that the analyst specifies should be asked in the same way (the same product concept formulation) for all respondents. In many CBC applications, choice tasks for estimating part-worth utilities are not fixed, but vary across respondents. Often, each respondent receives a randomly selected version of the choice tasks. This randomly selected version is intended to cover the domain of attribute levels and to be level-balanced and nearly orthogonal.

Fixed tasks are most often used as holdout tasks for checking internal validity. In other words, they are not used in estimating part-worths, but are used to check how well those part-worths can predict the share of choices observed for the fixed tasks. For example, a fixed choice task may be asked in the tenth choice task position in a twenty-task CBC questionnaire. The fixed choice task consistently displays the same product concept formulations to all respondents (perhaps a particular set of product alternatives of interest to the client), whereas the other nineteen choice tasks vary in composition across respondents. For the fixed holdout task, we might observe that 10 percent of the respondents chose concept 1, 60 percent chose concept 2, and 30 percent chose concept 3. If we specify a market simulation scenario using the same product concept definitions as the fixed task, we might obtain predicted values very close to those proportions. If so, we would feel more confident that the model was working well and that we had not made any serious errors in design or data processing. See fixed design and randomized design.

forced choice A discrete choice or choice-based conjoint question that does not include a *none* alternative. Respondents are thus forced to select from one of the available product alternatives.

fractional factorial With a conjoint analysis study, if there are six attributes each with four levels, there are $4^6 = 4096$ possible product concept realizations. What makes conjoint analysis work in practice is that it is usually not necessary to ask respondents to evaluate all possible product combinations. Typically, just a carefully selected fraction of the total possible combinations is needed to estimate the part-worth utility effects that account for the vast majority of the variation in respondents' product evaluations/choices. In the previous example, all 4096 possible combinations define the full factorial or complete design, whereas a carefully selected subset of these realizations (as an example, 32 out of 4096 combinations) is termed a fractional factorial or reduced design.

full factorial See related topic, fractional factorial.

full profile Also known as multiple factor evaluation or profile method. Describes a conjoint analysis approach in which a product concept is fully defined using one level from each of the attributes in the study. For example, if the researcher is studying six total attributes describing laptop computers, all six attributes are reflected in each product profile. A full-profile product concept may look like exhibit A.3.

Apple PowerBook
1.67 GHz processor
1 GB RAM
17-inch display
3-hour battery life
$2,694

Exhibit A.3. A full-profile concept

Many researchers favor full profiles because products are defined on all aspects, as they are in the real world. Most conjoint studies today, whether using ratings or choices of product concepts, employ full profiles. Despite the benefits of full profiles, many researchers argue that respondents may become confused or fatigued if they have to view product concepts involving more than about six attributes (though this certainly varies by respondents, attribute formulation, and subject matter). This confusion may result in respondents paying less attention to the variety of attributes they might really attend to in the real world, and may also encourage noncompensatory choice rules.

A partial profile involves the presentation of a subset of the attributes in a product concept. Adaptive Conjoint Analysis (ACA) uses partial-profile conjoint questions. Choice-based conjoint (CBC) can also be used in partial-profile mode. See also card-sort conjoint.

generic attribute An attribute (product feature) that is applicable to all product alternatives in a discrete choice experiment. The traditional choice-based conjoint (CBC) study uses generic attributes. For example, if studying purchases of laptop computers, the various attributes (e.g., screen size, installed software, RAM, and storage space) are applicable and present in all competing alternatives (brands) from different suppliers. In contrast, alternative-specific attributes are those that only apply to certain brands or product alternatives.

graded pairs A term usually describing the type of conjoint questions and preference scale used in Adaptive Conjoint Analysis (ACA) and also as an option in Sawtooth Software's CVA program. Graded pairs show two product concepts at a time and ask respondents to compare them using a sliding rating scale (a graded scale), often running from one to nine. See the example in exhibit A.4.

Which of these meals would you prefer?	
Shrimp cocktail Filet mignon Apple pie	Fresh fruit cup Roast chicken Vanilla ice cream
1 2 3 4 5 6 7 8 9 *Strongly Indifferent Strongly* *prefer prefer* *left right*	

Exhibit A.4. Graded pairs scale for menu preferences

Green, Paul Academic, leading researcher, and mentor in conjoint analysis at the Wharton School of the University of Pennsylvania. Paul Green was the first marketing professor to recognize that conjoint measurement (a theory forwarded in a mathematical psychology journal article) could be applied to marketing and business problems. Together with coauthor Rao, Green published the first article on conjoint analysis in the marketing literature in 1971. Since then, he has been the most prominent and oft-cited researcher in the conjoint analysis field.

HB See hierarchical Bayes.

heterogeneity Generally refers to differences in tastes and preferences among people. A data set including respondents that are quite different in terms of preferences is termed heterogeneous, as opposed to a homogeneous data set where people are very similar. Conjoint methods and preference estimation methods differ in terms of their ability to capture heterogeneity across respondents. Traditional conjoint analysis as developed in the early 1970s usually developed separate part-worth utility scores for each individual. Individual-level models offer the greatest opportunity to capture respondent heterogeneity, especially when each respondent answers many conjoint questions. Conjoint models that reflect heterogeneity often produce more accurate predictions than those that do not.

With discrete choice or choice-based conjoint (CBC) methods, the main estimation model available until the mid-1990s was aggregate logit, which pooled data across respondents, estimating a summary set of part-worth utilities for the sample. Aggregate models assume homogeneity and cannot distinguish true heterogeneity from random noise. Exceptions to that rule are aggregate models that incorporate observed respondent characteristics (such as gender, age, or income) as predictive variables (covariates).

hierarchical Bayes (HB) estimation A computationally intensive method that may be used for estimating part-worth utilities for conjoint and choice-based conjoint (discrete choice) experiments. Bayes theorem was forwarded by the Reverend Thomas Bayes in the 1700s. But estimating part-worth utilities for conjoint analysis using Bayes theorem only became feasible with the availability of fast computers, and by using simulated (Monte Carlo Markov Chain) processes such as Gibbs Sampling. Greg Allenby of the Ohio State University and various coauthors were very influential in promoting HB for the marketing research community, publishing papers as early as 1995 on the use of HB in conjoint analysis and later teaching HB tutorials at the American Marketing Association's Advanced Research Techniques Forum. In 1999, Sawtooth Software marketed the first commercial HB software for choice-based conjoint analysis (CBC/HB).

HB made it possible to estimate reasonably stable individual-level part-worth utilities from choice-based conjoint data, whereas stable estimates could only be achieved previously by pooling many respondents in group analysis. HB also was beneficial for ratings-based conjoint methods (such as Adaptive Conjoint Analysis and traditional full-profile conjoint analysis), leading to more precise and accurate part-worths.

The term "hierarchical" refers to separate lower- and upper-level models for the data. In the lower-level model, HB considers how well part-worth utilities fit each respondent's choices or ratings. In the upper-level model, HB estimates overall part-worth utility averages and variances for the sample population, including the covariances between part-worths across the respondents. The idea behind how HB improves individual respondent estimation is that it borrows information from other respondents in the sample to stabilize the estimates for each individual. To the degree that respondents are quite consistent in their responses, less is borrowed from the population characteristics. When respondents are less consistent, or quite atypical, more information is borrowed from population characteristics to shrink them toward the mean and stabilize their part-worths.

hit rate A measure of the ability of conjoint analysis to predict individual responses to holdout profiles. For example, a respondent may have completed eighteen choice tasks in a choice-based conjoint experiment, followed by another choice task that is held out for validation purposes (not used in the estimation of part-worth utilities). Using the part-worth utilities developed from the first eighteen choice tasks, one predicts responses to the holdout choice task. If the prediction matches the respondent's choice, a hit is recorded for this respondent. If not, a miss is recorded. The hit rate across the sample is the percent of correctly predicted holdout responses using the model.

Hit rates for holdout choice tasks involving three or four product alternatives usually range from 70 to 85 percent. Many researchers use hit rates to compare conjoint methods or different models using the same conjoint method. But this measure of success is typically not as meaningful to management as the accuracy of share predictions from market simulators, measured in terms of mean absolute error or mean squared error. Successful conjoint models feature both high hit rates and excellent share prediction accuracy. See holdout, internal validity, mean absolute error, and mean squared error.

holdout Refers to conjoint or discrete choice (CBC) questions not used to estimate part-worth utilities, but held out separately to assess the quality or performance of the estimated part-worths. If the responses to held-out questions can be predicted accurately using estimated part-worths, it lends greater credibility to the model. Assessing the quality of part-worth estimation using holdout questions is more indicative of internal reliability than of predictive validity. True validity tests usually require real-world sales or choice data rather than holdout conjoint questions asked during the same survey as the other conjoint tasks. See external validity, fixed tasks, and internal validity.

hybrid conjoint analysis This term most often refers to the combination of self-explicated preference measurement and conjoint questions within the same questionnaire and model. The final part-worth utilities reflect a weighted combination of the two types of preference information. Hybrid conjoint methods were designed for situations in which the number of attributes and levels exceeded the reasonable capacities of traditional full-profile conjoint analysis. Paul Green published papers describing his hybrid conjoint approach, and Richard Johnson's Adaptive Conjoint Analysis (ACA) may be thought of as a hybrid conjoint method. See related topic, self-explicated approach.

ideal point model Also known as quadratic model. With some attributes, like the temperature of coffee or the amount of sweetener in a soft drink, each individual prefers a specific, ideal amount. Not hot enough or too hot is a bad thing when it comes to coffee. Some conjoint researchers have preferred to model such preference functions with an ideal point model represented by a smooth quadratic curve. See figure A.1.

Fitting a curve to a utility function (rather than separately estimating the preference at each discrete temperature level) requires just two estimated parameters, potentially smoothing noisy data and reducing the tendency to overfit. Very few analysts today employ ideal point utility functions for attributes. The part-worth model is generally preferred.

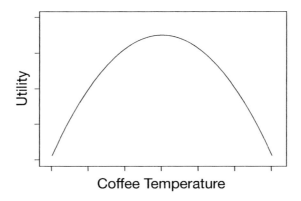

Figure A.1. Ideal point utility function

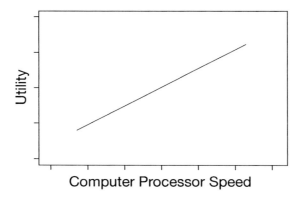

Figure A.2. Ideal vector model

ideal vector model   With some continuous attributes like price or speed, more or less is always better. If the relationship between the numeric levels of the attribute and the utility is close to linear, some researchers prefer to fit a single linear coefficient, or slope, to the data. This is known as an ideal vector model.

Consider an ideal vector model for computer processor speed, for which higher speeds are always preferred to lower speeds. Fitting a line to a utility function (rather than separately estimating the preference at each discrete level of speed) requires just one estimated parameter, potentially smoothing noisy data and reducing the tendency to overfit. The drawback is that, if the functional form is not truly linear, the model may have lower fit. See exhibit A.2.

IIA   See independence from irrelevant alternatives.

importance   The maximum impact an attribute can exert upon product choice. Attribute importance generally is calculated by finding the percentage of the range in utilities (maximum less minimum utility) across attributes. See exhibit A.5 for the calculation of importances from an individual's part-worth utilities.

Importance provides a summary measure that is easy to compute and has intuitive meaning, but without appropriate reference to the specific attribute levels involved, an importance means very little. The importances are directly related to the attribute level ranges that the analyst used in the experiment. If we had included a wider range of prices in exhibit A.5, the importance of the price attribute would have been greater. For this reason, if importance scores are presented to management, it is advisable to show the attribute levels involved. Some analysts avoid showing management importance scores, given the real possibility of misuse. Importance

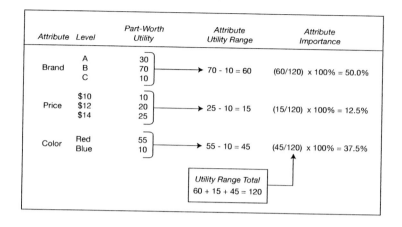

Exhibit A.5. Calculation of importance from part-worth utility

numbers have a way of taking on a life of their own, and the underlying reference levels are soon forgotten.

Some researchers prefer to show attribute impact in terms of sensitivity analysis. Sensitivity analysis has the further benefit of distinguishing random noise from an attribute's real impact. An attribute with no significant effect on choice (where the part-worths reflect random noise) will always have positive importance if importance is defined simply as the difference between the best and worst levels. However, random noise cancels out over many respondents within sensitivity simulations, so such an attribute would not receive an inflated measure of attribute impact.

Some researchers use the term "importance" when they mean to say "preference." It is not correct to refer to the desirability of a single attribute level as importance—it is preference or utility (part-worth utility). See sensitivity analysis.

independence from irrelevant alternatives Referred to as IIA and commonly known as the "red bus/blue bus problem." A property of the logit model, in which the ratio of any two product alternatives' shares is constant, irrespective of changes to (or introductions of) other product alternatives. As an illustration of the IIA property, consider only two available beverages in a market: Coke and milk. Further assume that Coke captures 80 percent of the market and milk 20 percent (i.e., Coke's share is four times that of milk). Assume Pepsi, a new competitor, enters the market and captures 50 percent share. According to the IIA property, Pepsi would take share proportionally (at a constant substitution rate) from Coke and milk, such that the resulting shares would be Coke 40 percent, milk 10 percent, and Pepsi 50 percent. That is, after the introduction of Pepsi, the ratio of Coke's to milk's shares would still be four to one, but milk's share would be cut from 20 percent to 10 percent.

While the IIA property makes logit models very efficient computationally, most researchers regard it as quite unrealistic. One would expect that the introduction of Pepsi would take share principally from Coke, leaving milk's share essentially unchanged. A common illustration of the same principle involves highly substitutable options for getting to work (a red bus and a blue bus) versus other dissimilar alternatives like driving, biking, and walking—hence, the "red bus/blue bus problem." The good news for market researchers is that when using individual-level estimation of part-worths and the logit simulation model, the IIA trouble is greatly reduced. Within each individual, the IIA property still holds. But, when simulated choices for each individual are accumulated across the population, the overall results reflect more realistic substitution patterns among similar products rather than strictly following the IIA property.

Some researchers deal with IIA troubles by using different model formulations such as nested logit or models that incorporate availability effects. See multinomial logit and share of preference.

interaction effect Typical conjoint analysis models assume that the utility of a product alternative is equal to the sum of the values of its independent parts. However, there are situations in which the levels from two attributes combine to create something considerably better or worse than their independent values might suggest. Such a case is termed an interaction. For example, if we are studying automobiles, the combination of convertible with the color red may produce a synergistic effect upon utility that is not explainable by the preferences for the separate values of models and colors. Also, if limousine is combined with the color red, that combination is considerably worse than might be expected from the separate utility scores for red and limousine. Interaction effects are parameters that are estimated in addition to the main attribute level effects (main effects).

interattribute correlation See environmental correlation.

internal validity Refers to the ability of a conjoint analysis model or market simulator to accurately predict some additional choice or conjoint question not used in the estimation of part-worth utilities, such as a holdout question. Internal validity is a less demanding standard than external validity, which characterizes the model's ability to predict events outside the survey, such as actual market purchases. See external validity and holdout.

Johnson, Richard Influential practitioner and software developer who founded Sawtooth Software in 1983, after having worked at Procter & Gamble, Market Facts, and John Morton Company (which he cofounded). Johnson received his Ph.D. in Psychometrics from the University of Washington.

He is credited with inventing trade-off matrices (Johnson 1974) and Adaptive Conjoint Analysis (ACA) (Johnson 1987b). He also published many influential articles on conjoint analysis and organized the Sawtooth Software conferences.

latent class analysis Also known as finite mixture model. A model and estimation technique for analyzing discrete choice (CBC) data that finds groups (classes) of respondents that exhibit similar choice patterns and develops a set of part-worth utilities for each class. Like cluster analysis, the analyst specifies how many groups to model, and the technique finds relatively homogeneous groups where the individuals' preferences are similar within groups and dissimilar between groups. Unlike cluster analysis, latent class analysis is model driven in that a solution is found subject to independent variables (variations in attributes) best predicting respondent choices for product concepts. The fit is often measured in terms of likelihood, and a multinomial logit model is developed within each group. In latent class analysis, all respondents within each group are assumed to have identical preferences, except for random noise. Respondents are not discretely assigned to groups (as in cluster analysis), but have probabilities of membership in each group.

Latent class analysis is valuable for discovering needs-based segments. Latent class models also generally perform better than aggregate logit models, both in terms of fit and predictive validity, given the same model specification. See heterogeneity, likelihood, and multinomial logit.

least squares See ordinary least squares.

level A degree or amount of an attribute. For example, levels for the attribute brand may be Coke, Pepsi, and Sprite. Levels of price might be $10, $15, and $20. Every attribute in conjoint analysis must have at least two levels. Levels should have concrete meaning, and be mutually exclusive within each attribute, meaning a product concept is defined using one and only one level of each attribute.

level balance A desirable property for conjoint designs that levels within the same attribute should appear an equal number of times in the questionnaire. Some orthogonal arrays published in design catalogs or produced by design software lack level balance and are suboptimal. Computer search routines that pay attention to both level balance and orthogonality can produce designs that lead to more precise estimates of part-worth utilities for levels, even though they may sacrifice a small degree of orthogonality.

level overlap Refers to whether an attribute level (such as a particular brand, speed, or color) repeats across alternatives within the same choice task in CBC. For example, with three levels of brand, if three product alternatives (concepts) are shown per choice task, each brand can be represented exactly once per choice task. This would reflect no level overlap with respect to brand. If four product alternatives were displayed per choice set, one of the brands would need to be repeated, causing some level overlap. Repeating a level within a choice task only after all levels within the same attribute have been used is termed minimal overlap. Minimal overlap strategies are most efficient with respect to main effects estimation, assuming respondents apply compensatory (simple additivity) decision rules.

lexicographic choice rule A noncompensatory evaluation heuristic for choosing among complex products or services. First, the respondent/buyer ranks (orders) the attributes in terms of importance. Next, product alternatives are compared based only on the attribute of most importance. If one alternative exceeds the others on this most important aspect, it is selected. If there is a tie in terms of performance on this most important attribute, then the tied product alternatives are compared on the next most important attribute, etc. The lexicographic choice rule is one of many kinds of simplification strategies that respondents may employ to deal with the challenge of choosing among many complex competitive offerings. Conjoint analysis models usually assume a compensatory (additive) rule, where negative aspects of a product may be compensated for by other desirable qualities. Additive models, therefore, may have some difficulty fitting the data well if many respondents consistently use noncompensatory choice processes. See additivity, conjunctive choice rule, elimination-by-aspects choice rule, and unacceptables.

likelihood A measure of fit used in choice-based conjoint (CBC), indicating the probability that the observed choices would have resulted given the estimated part-worths. For example, if a given set of part-worth utilities suggest that there is a probability of 0.60 that a given respondent will pick alternative A in a CBC question and the respondent indeed picks A, the likelihood or fit to the data for that task is 0.60. As respondents usually complete more than one choice task, likelihoods are computed across multiple choice tasks. If the predicted probabilities of choice (given the part-worths for an individual) for the alternatives actually chosen in choice tasks one, two, and three are 0.60, 0.40, and 0.90, respectively, the likelihood for the estimated part-worth model is equal to the product of the likelihoods across the tasks, or $(0.60)(0.40)(0.90) = 0.216$.

Multiplying probabilities across many choice tasks and respondents results in extremely tiny numbers near zero, so the logs of the likelihoods are accumulated across tasks and respondents to summarize model fit to choices. Log-likelihoods are negative values, where the best possible log-likelihood fit (assuming 1.00 probability for all choice tasks across the sample) is zero.

likelihood of purchase See purchase likelihood.

LINMAP Early part-worth utility estimation program appropriate for rank-order (card-sort or nonmetric) data. Developed by Srinivasan and Shocker (1973).

log-likelihood See likelihood.

logit See multinomial logit.

Louviere, Jordan Prominent academic and researcher in the area of discrete choice analysis. Jordan applied theories developed by McFadden in the early 1970s to marketing research problems, publishing an important paper on the design and analysis of choice experiments, together with Woodward, in 1983. Jordan's career has spanned academia and work in private consultancies and firms. He is also credited with inventing the MaxDiff technique for scaling multiple items.

macro/micro conjoint Sometimes, conjoint researchers wish to study the most fundamental (macro) aspects of a product alternative. For example, a study of tractors might consider brand, price, capacity, engine size, economy, durability, and sophistication of the cab. Additionally, the researcher may be interested in creating a separate conjoint interview to examine in-depth a detailed (micro) aspect of the overall product concept, such as the sophistication of the cab, which is one of the attributes within the macro attribute list. The micro attribute list might focus on a number of attributes related to the specific instrumentation layout within the tractor's cab. The results from the macro and micro conjoint designs are sometimes bridged together, based on the utility range for the relevant macro attribute. Sometimes the results are analyzed separately.

MAE See mean absolute error.

main effect The independent preference or utility for the attribute levels, holding all other attributes constant. For example, consider the following attributes, levels, and main effect part-worth utilities:

Attribute	Level	Utility
Brand	Coke	0.20
	Pepsi	0.00
	7-Up	-0.20
Price	$2.50	0.40
	$2.75	0.10
	$3.00	-0.50

With main effects, the effect (utility) of brand is estimated independent of price (and vice versa). We interpret the part-worths above to indicate that, holding price constant, Coke is preferred to Pepsi, and Pepsi is preferred to 7-Up. The part-worth utilities for price reflect the average price sensitivity across all brands (holding brand constant).

Main effects ignore the possibility of interactions between attributes. If interactions exist (and are not accounted for), main effect estimates are biased.

market share Most conjoint practitioners use the term "market share" to refer to actual purchases (usually percent of volume) made by buyers in real markets. Academics sometimes refer to the share predictions from conjoint market simulators as market shares as well. Practitioners prefer to apply the term "shares of preference" to the predictions from conjoint market simulators in recognition that only under controlled situations will the predicted shares of preference closely match actual market shares. There are many other factors not incorporated in the conjoint model that shape market shares in the real world, such as distribution, awareness, effectiveness of sales force, and time on the market. See related topics, external effects and external validity.

market simulator Also known as choice simulator. Using the part-worth utilities estimated from conjoint analysis experiments, researchers can build what-if simulators to predict how the market would choose among a set of competing product alternatives. For example, the researcher might consider four competing product alternatives, each with its own brand, color, speed, and price. For each individual, one first calculates the total utility that the competing products achieve. The most simple form of market simulator predicts that each individual chooses or buys the product alternative that has the highest utility. The projected choices for the product alternatives are accumulated across respondents to indicate shares of preference. The shares are usually scaled to sum to 100 percent. For example, with four product alternatives, the market simulation results might look like this:

Product	Share of Preference Percentage
A	30
B	12
C	15
D	43
	Total = 100

In the typical application, every respondent is expected to be in the market and choose at least one of the offerings, so the shares of preference sum to 100%. What-if games can be played by modifying the features of one (or more) of the products (such as modifying the speed or the price) and rerunning the market simulator to see how the shares of preference change.

Market simulators are also useful because they convert part-worth utilities, which are difficult for managers to interpret, into shares of preference, which are easily interpreted and have clear strategic meaning. They are useful managerial tools for estimating the impact of product modifications, product introductions, and line extensions.

When choosing a place to live, which of the following factors is most and least important to you?

Most Important		Least Important
O	*Location/neighborhood*	O
O	*Monthly rent or mortgage*	O
O	*Availability of parking*	O
O	*Proximity to shopping*	O

Exhibit A.6. MaxDiff question format

MaxDiff See maximum difference scaling.

maximum difference scaling Also known as MaxDiff and best/worst scaling. Invented by Jordan Louviere in the late 1980s, MaxDiff is a technique for obtaining preference or importance scores for a set of items, where the items may be brands, product features, performance attributes, or political positions, for example. In MaxDiff, respondents are typically shown choice sets involving four to six items at a time. In each set, respondents indicate which item is best and worst. See exhibit A.6.

Compared to the standard ratings scale approach in which respondents assign ratings to each item, the MaxDiff approach has been shown to increase discrimination among items and between respondents on the items. It has also been shown to produce more accurate predictions of choice versus standard ratings (Cohen 2003). Although MaxDiff may be considered a trade-off technique, it is not a conjoint method because respondents do not evaluate the desirability of attribute levels considered jointly. Rather, respondents are asked to contrast individual items or attribute levels, where each item is in competition with the other (instead of having items combined in a product whole).

maximum likelihood estimation A method for estimating part-worth utilities or coefficients where the goal is to maximize the fit to respondents' choices (usually in a CBC questionnaire) in terms of likelihood. See likelihood for further discussion.

maximum utility rule See first-choice model.

mean absolute error Known by the acronym MAE. A summary measure of fit for predictions of shares for product alternatives. As an example, see exhibit A.7. There are three choice alternatives, A, B, and C, with the following choice probabilities (percent of respondents actually choosing each alternative) of 50, 20, and 30 percent, respectively. Consider a market simulation model based on conjoint analysis data that yields predictions of choice for those same product alternatives as 46, 22, and 32 percent, respectively. The exhibit shows the absolute errors of prediction (differences between predicted and actual results) for each alternative. The MAE is the average of those errors of prediction across the product alternatives. MAE is expressed in the original units of measure of the input data.

The lower the MAE, the better the model fit. The absolute size of the MAE is directly related to the number of alternatives in the choice scenario. With more alternatives, the MAE tends to be lower. See mean squared error.

mean squared error Also known as MSE. Like mean absolute error, this is a measure of model fit in predicting shares of preference or market shares for product alternatives. Mean squared error is the average of the squared errors of prediction. Some researchers prefer to use the mean squared error rather than the mean absolute error. The mean squared error penalizes larger misses more heavily than does the mean absolute error. Note also, that MSE is expressed in squared units, whereas MAE is expressed in the original units of measure of the input data. See exhibit A.8. See mean absolute error.

MNL See multinomial logit.

MONONOVA Early (1960s) estimation program appropriate for rank-order (card-sort or nonmetric) data developed by Kruskal.

monotonicity Consistently increasing or decreasing desirability for levels across the attribute range.

monotonicity constraints See constraints.

mother logit model A multinomial logit (MNL) model that includes all main effects plus all cross-alternative effects. These models sometimes include hundreds of parameters to estimate. The only way to stabilize estimates of large numbers of parameters is to pool data across respondents in an aggregate model. The cross-effect terms are able to account for many IIA violations. Mother logit models have lost popularity as analytical methods such as latent class analysis and hierarchical Bayes (HB) are able to resolve many IIA difficulties using more parsimonious models that represent respondent heterogeneity. Mother logit models are more challenging to build and explain to management, often include many coefficients that are nonsignificant, may lack face validity, and risk overfitting. See cross-effects, independence from irrelevant alternatives, multinomial logit, and overfitting.

MSE See mean squared error.

Choice Alternative	Actual Choice Percentage	Predicted Choice Percentage	Error Percentage	Absolute Error Percentage
A	50	46	4	4
B	20	22	-2	2
C	30	32	-2	2

MAE = (4 + 2 + 2)/3 = 2.67

(expressed in original units of measure, percentage in this example)

Exhibit A.7. Calculating mean absolute error

Choice Alternative	Actual Choice Percentage	Predicted Choice Percentage	Error Percentage	Squared Error Percentage
A	50	46	4	16
B	20	22	-2	4
C	30	32	-2	4

MSE = (16 + 4 + 4)/3 = 8

(expressed in original squared units of measure, squared percentage in this example)

Exhibit A.8. Calculating mean squared error

multinomial logit Also known as MNL. A multivariate statistical model for re-
lating utilities to probabilities of choice. Multinomial logit is often used for
estimating part-worth utilities based on discrete choice (CBC) questionnaires involving multiple product alternatives per choice task. A multinomial logit model fits a set of part-worth utilities (often referred to as
effects within the logit framework) to the data, either across many respondents or for an individual respondent, such that the choices actually made
are most faithfully predicted according to the logit rule (described below).
The fit statistic that is maximized is called the likelihood. (See maximum
likelihood estimation.) The logit model holds that the probability that an
individual will choose product alternative a from choice set $\{a, b, c\}$ is

$$P_a = \frac{e^{U_a}}{(e^{U_a} + e^{U_b} + e^{U_c})}$$

For example, if the utilities for alternatives a, b, and c for an individual
are 0.5, 0.4, and -0.1, respectively, then the probability of this individual
choosing product a is

$$P_a = \frac{e^{0.5}}{(e^{0.5} + e^{0.4} + e^{-0.1})} = 0.407$$

and the probabilities of choosing alternatives b and c are

$$P_b = \frac{e^{0.4}}{(e^{0.5} + e^{0.4} + e^{-0.1})} = 0.369$$

$$P_c = \frac{e^{-0.1}}{(e^{0.5} + e^{0.4} + e^{-0.1})} = 0.224$$

The predicted choice probabilities across available alternatives add to 1.00.
e^{U_i} is synonymous with taking the antilog of U_i, or exponentiating U_i. In
Excel, the formula "=exp(0.4)" is used to indicate $e^{0.4}$.

The multinomial logit model is often used in pooling or aggregating across
respondents so that estimates of part-worth utility parameters can be sta-
bilized. Obtaining an aggregate solution based only on product characteristics ignores differences across respondents (heterogeneity), and such aggregate logit models are quite subject to IIA difficulties. See heterogeneity
and IIA for more detail.

Latent class analysis, when applied to choice data, also uses the multinomial logit model to estimate part-worth utilities for each class of respondents. Latent class models are less susceptible to IIA problems. More
recently, advances in hierarchical Bayes analysis have permitted the multinomial logit model to be used in the estimation of part-worth utilities for
individual respondents. These individual-level multinomial logit models
are even less susceptible to IIA problems than latent class models.

multiple regression See ordinary least squares regression.

multi-store simulator A market simulation approach for appropriately adjusting market simulators to account for an unequal distribution of products across the market, without changing their original price sensitivities or substitution rates (Orme and Johnson 2006). A multi-store simulator allows the researcher to specify, in the simplest case, the percentage of the regions/stores that carry each product. Superior implementations specify which specific products are available within each region/store and how much volume each region/store accounts for. Respondents are then randomly selected (with probability proportional to store volume) to make simulated visits to multiple stores on each of hundreds or thousands of occasions and to make choices among available products.

If the respondent's location is known, the respondent can be assigned to visit the applicable regional store or stores, rather than using a random process. The multi-store simulator is not just a tool for adjusting simulated shares to better reflect availability of products across the market (and, in turn, market shares), but it more directly accounts for substitution effects by recognizing which products directly compete with one another (because they tend to be offered within the same regions/stores).

must-haves Product features that a respondent indicates must be present for a product to be considered for purchase. When respondents apply *must-have* rules, the assumption that the respondent follows a simple compensatory model is violated. The assumption of compensatory decision-making underlies traditional conjoint analysis and discrete choice. The idea of *must-haves* implies unacceptables. If an attribute carries a *must-have* level, the other levels within the same attribute are, in turn, unacceptable. Leading researchers (Gilbride and Allenby 2004; Hauser et al. 2006; Johnson and Orme 2007) suggest that many respondents make choices in CBC questionnaires consistent with applying *must-have* rules. Questionnaires and analytical techniques used by these authors, such as the method of adaptive choice-based conjoint proposed by Johnson and Orme (2007), directly incorporate the notion of must-haves. See adaptive choice-based conjoint, conjunctive choice rule, unacceptables.

NOL See number-of-levels effect.

nominal attribute See categorical attribute.

noncompensatory rule See conjunctive choice rule, elimination-by-aspects choice rule, lexicographic choice rule, and unacceptables.

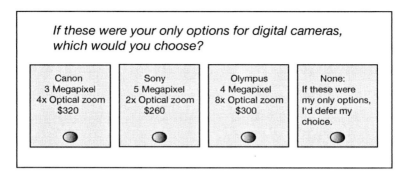

If these were your only options for digital cameras, which would you choose?

Canon	Sony	Olympus	None:
3 Megapixel	5 Megapixel	4 Megapixel	If these were
4x Optical zoom	2x Optical zoom	8x Optical zoom	my only options,
$320	$260	$300	I'd defer my
			choice.

Exhibit A.9. Choice-based conjoint example with *none* concept

***none* concept** In choice-based conjoint, researchers often allow respondents to say that they would choose none of the product concepts if these were the only ones available. The *none* concept is a type of constant alternative. Consider a choice task involving digital cameras in which the fourth concept is *none*. See exhibit A.9.

Allowing the respondent to indicate *none* better mimics real-world choice, in which respondents generally are not forced to buy anything. Including the *none* concept is often a good thing to do, but a choice of *none* contributes much less information for refining part-worth utility estimates of the levels of interest than a selection of a product concept.

The *none* alternative allows the researcher to simulate whether respondents would choose from the category at all, given the product characteristics and prices included in the market scenario. For example, if all of the products offered are priced too high, many buyers would not purchase any of the alternatives. Although this is a noted benefit for including a *none* alternative, many researchers are skeptical whether the *none* choices recorded in the choice experiment are actually representative of a lack of demand in the real marketplace. The propensity to choose *none* may be affected by task complexity, number of alternatives in the choice task, and respondent fatigue. Many researchers, therefore, prefer to include the *none* option in choice questionnaires but subsequently ignore the parameter during market simulations.

null level The blank or "off" level, typically associated with binary (on/off) attributes in conjoint analysis. For example, in an automobile features study, the sunroof attribute may be formulated with two levels: no sunroof or sunroof. The "no sunroof" level is the null (nothing) condition. The null level is often left blank, so that nothing is displayed on the screen for that level. Null levels can also occur with attributes involving more than just two levels. The above example for automobile features could be expanded to consider an eight-level composite factor accounting for combinations of sunroof, GPS system, and DVD video system:

- Null (blank level)
- Sunroof included
- GPS navigation system included
- DVD video system included
- Sunroof, GPS navigation system included
- Sunroof, DVD video system included
- GPS navigation, DVD video system included
- Sunroof, GPS navigation, and DVD video system included

number-of-levels effect Also known as NOL. If an attribute is defined using more, rather than fewer, levels (holding the range of variation in the attribute constant), the number-of-levels effect is manifest, and the attribute takes on increased attribute importance. As an example, assume that we were to define a price attribute using just two levels: $10 and $16, and that the results of the conjoint experiment indicate that price captures 20% relative importance. If we repeated the study, holding all other attributes constant, but this time defined price with four levels: $10, $12, $14, and $16, we would observe larger relative importance for price, even though the total range in price variation was held constant from $10 to $16. The effect can be demonstrated for attributes other than price and has been a cause of concern over the years for conjoint analysts.

The number-of-levels effect is probably due to both psychological and algorithmic issues. It is more problematic for choice-based conjoint and full-profile conjoint analysis than for Adaptive Conjoint Analysis.

observation In conjoint analysis, each respondent almost always provides multiple observations, where an observation is defined as a rating for (or choice of) a product concept. For example, a respondent who rates eighteen product profiles (concepts) is said to provide eighteen observations.

OLS See ordinary least squares regression.

order bias A situation in which the order of presentation of attributes in conjoint (or MaxDiff) questions has a significant effect upon estimated part-worth utilities or preference scores. For example, if respondents tend to pay more attention to attributes/items listed at the top of the product concept, this can lead to biased (overweighted) attention toward these attributes. Generally, one would be concerned that respondents might tend to pay undue attention to attributes at the top and potentially the bottom of lists as well.

A few studies have been published reporting whether significant order bias occurs in conjoint analysis. Most studies have found significant (albeit modest) order effects, though the pattern of bias is not consistent. To control for order bias, researchers can randomize the presentation order of attributes. This comes at the risk of sacrificing task realism, as products in the real world are often described in specific attribute orders. In such cases, we would favor realism over attempts to control for order bias. See positional balance.

ordered attribute An attribute whose levels have rational a priori preference order, meaning we know ahead of time the rank order of preference. Ordered attributes can be either continuous, such as price or speed, or categorical, such as the following levels of service: (1) no free service, support, or product upgrades, (2) free service and technical support, (3) free service, technical support, and product upgrades. In the example levels above, we know that level 3 should be preferred to level 2, and level 2 should be preferred to level 1. See a priori and constraint.

ordinary least squares regression Also known as OLS or multiple regression. A statistical estimation method for predicting some outcome y or dependent variable using a linear combination of independent variables x_1 to x_n. An optimal set of weights (betas) for the independent variables is found, which minimize the sums of the squares of the differences between the predicted and the actual outcomes.

OLS estimation is often used to estimate part-worth utilities for ratings-based conjoint questionnaires. The product attributes are the independent variables, and the ratings for the product concepts make up the dependent variable.

orthogonality A statistical term that, when applied to conjoint analysis experimental designs, refers to experiments in which the attributes are uncorrelated across product concepts. In more technical terms, the columns in the design matrix have zero correlation between levels of different attributes. Independence of attributes is important to conjoint analysis studies because it allows the researcher to estimate each part-worth utility independent of the levels of other attributes in the model. Orthogonality allows separate estimation for each attribute independent of the others, but it does not, by itself, guarantee precision. Orthogonal designs were very popular for many years in conjoint analysis. Particularly since the 1990s, researchers have learned that orthogonal designs are not necessarily the best option. Here are some reasons:

- Orthogonal designs are quite inflexible with regard to how many conjoint questions should be shown, so it is difficult to choose precisely the number of questions that is right for respondents and that provides the desired degrees of freedom.

- For conjoint studies in which the numbers of levels differ across attributes, orthogonal designs are sometimes not balanced, meaning that some attribute levels can appear more times than others. When this occurs, the more frequently occurring levels are measured with greater precision than the less frequent levels within the same attribute.

- Orthogonal designs often yield product concepts or comparisons among product concepts that are quite unrealistic or for which there is a clear winner or dominant alternative. Such situations are usually not desirable in conjoint analysis surveys, and designs that sacrifice a modest degree of orthogonality have the potential to produce better overall results.

overfitting When additional parameters added to a model are not truly useful, they can harm the predictive accuracy of out-of-sample observations. Sometimes researchers try to estimate many parameters in a conjoint/choice model, where parameters may refer to (among other things) part-worths, linear coefficients, interaction terms, and cross-effects. Also, researchers may attempt to estimate separate parameters for individuals or many latent groups (as in latent class) using sparse data. Capturing heterogeneity, it can be argued, means fitting additional parameters into the model (a set of terms for each group or individual). In all these cases, the researcher may face the problem of overfitting. Whenever one adds additional explanatory (independent) variables to the model, the fit to the conjoint or choice tasks used for estimation increases. The fit improves because the estimation method takes advantage of the new parameters to account for as-of-yet unexplained variance. The danger is that, although the addition of new parameters improves the fit to the observations used for estimation, the additional parameters are not truly useful, and the resulting model may be less predictive of new out-of-sample observations (such as holdouts or real market purchases).

overlap See level overlap.

paired comparisons The method of paired comparisons is a very old research technique for estimating the relative desirability or importance of items, brands, features, flavors, political candidates, and other stimulus objects. The technique involves showing items two at a time and asking the respondent to choose between them. For example, with four items, A, B, C, and D there are six possible paired comparisons: A versus B, A versus C, A versus D, B versus C, B versus D, and C versus D. With large numbers of items, the number of possible comparisons becomes quite large. If there are k items, the number of paired comparisons is given by

$$n = \frac{k(k-1)}{2}$$

In practice, researchers often ask respondents to evaluate a carefully chosen subset of the possible comparisons.

Adaptive Conjoint Analysis (ACA) users sometimes refer to the pairs section in ACA interviews as paired comparisons, though these really represent a different technique than the classic method of paired comparisons. See pairs.

pairs This term refers to showing two objects (attributes, brands, or product concepts) at a time and asking respondents to choose between them. Among Adaptive Conjoint Analysis users, the pairs section is the conjoint portion of the interview, in which respondents are asked to evaluate two competing product concepts typically defined by two to five attributes in partial profile. Respondents use a sliding rating scale to evaluate the concepts. See graded pairs for an example.

Sawtooth Software's CVA system for traditional full-profile conjoint analysis can also use pairs presentation. With CVA, the product profiles are always shown in full-profile (all attributes present in every question) and the survey is not adaptive. See conjoint value analysis, full profile, graded pairs, and paired comparisons.

Pareto-optimal designs Conjoint analysis questionnaires in which no one product concept is clearly superior (or inferior) to all other concepts on all attributes.

part-worth The utility associated with a particular level of an attribute in a multi-attribute conjoint analysis model. The total utility for the product is made up of the part-worths of its separate attributes (components). Sometimes researchers have referred to part-worths somewhat incorrectly as utilities. More technically, utilities refer to the total desirability of the product alternative, and part-worths refer to the component of desirability derived from the separate attribute levels for that product. See part-worth utility function.

part-worth utility function Also known as partial benefit value model. A model of preference in which the utility for each level of an attribute is measured independently of the others using dummy or effects coding. For an attribute like color, we might estimate the preference for four separate color levels. In figure A.3, we connect the separate part-worth utility values for each color with lines, even though it does not make sense to have an in-between color. But preferences for levels of quantitative attributes, such as price, weight, and speed, are also commonly estimated using part-worth utility functions. In these cases, it is usually reasonable to interpolate between two levels to estimate preference for a price that was never shown to respondents.

The part-worth utility function is the most commonly used approach today for conjoint and choice experiments. It has the benefit of not imposing a functional form, such as a linear or quadratic form, on the data when that assumption may not provide the best fit (see Ideal Vector Model, Ideal Point Model). However, part-worth models require more parameters to estimate and, in some cases, can lead to overfitting. See dummy coding, effects coding, and overfitting.

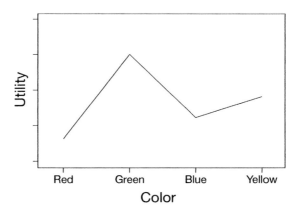

Figure A.3. Part-worth utility function

partial profile A partial profile involves the presentation of a subset of the attributes in a product concept. Adaptive Conjoint Analysis (ACA) uses partial-profile conjoint questions. Choice-based conjoint (CBC) can also be used in partial-profile mode. See full profile.

polytomous attribute See categorical attribute.

pooled analysis See aggregate model.

positional balance When conjoint or MaxDiff questions are displayed, multiple attributes (or items) are usually arranged vertically with attributes A, B, and C in the first, second, and third positions, respectively:

> Attribute A text
> Attribute B text
> Attribute C text
> ...

Order bias is a concern because respondents may pay more attention to attributes in the first position, for example. To control for order bias, we can randomize the order in which attributes are shown. When each item appears an equal number of items in each attribute position across tasks in the questionnaire, we have positional balance. See order bias.

priors In Adaptive Conjoint Analysis (ACA) priors refer to the self-explicated part-worth utilities that result from the level ratings/rankings and attribute importance questions at the beginning of the interview. In ACA, the priors are updated (refined) by adding information from the conjoint pairs that follow. The final utilities from ACA (OLS estimation) represent a weighted combination of the priors and pairs information.

The term *priors* is often used in hierarchical Bayes (HB) estimation, where it refers to prior knowledge of the part-worth utilities, variances, and covariances among attribute parameters. Usually, default priors assume that the part-worth utilities are zero, and that attribute parameters have equal variances, with covariances of zero. The priors are updated by referring to each respondent's product choices or product evaluations. The final part-worth utilities (posterior part-worth estimates) reflect good fit to the data, conditioned (influenced) by the priors. With HB, the more data available within each individual, the less the influence of the priors have upon the final part-worth estimates.

profile See concept.

prohibition Also known as restriction. When researchers design conjoint questionnaires, they might prohibit a certain level of one attribute from appearing with a certain level of another attribute within the same product profile. For example, one might prohibit a limousine from ever appearing in a red color. Some researchers have employed across-concept prohibitions, in which, for example, one price level is never to occur in comparison with another price level within the same choice task.

Prohibitions can lead to greater realism, but will have negative consequences on statistical design efficiency, and may lead to significantly lower precision for the part-worth utilities of attributes involved in the prohibitions. But modest prohibitions in some cases may actually lead to benefits that outweigh the negative effects of the loss in statistical efficiency. The benefits include added realism and the fact that the preference for certain levels (such as for color) are only estimated with respect to relevant other levels (such as car models). See composite factor.

purchase likelihood Generally refers to respondents' self-reported or stated likelihood that they will buy a given product concept at some future time. Purchase likelihood scales are often employed in traditional full-profile ratings-based conjoint analysis. They are also used in the optional "calibration concept" section in Adaptive Conjoint Analysis. Purchase likelihood is most typically asked on a 0- to 100-point scale. But 10-point scales, or even 5-point Likert scales (5=definitely would purchase, 4=probably would purchase, 3=might or might not purchase, 2=probably would not purchase, 1=definitely would not purchase) are sometimes used. Respondents are notoriously poor at estimating their purchase likelihoods and typically will exaggerate purchase intent.

Purchase likelihood is also the name of a market simulation model in Sawtooth Software's market simulator. This model transforms the utility for a product concept (defined using a level from each attribute in the study) into a relative purchase likelihood score from 0 to 100. No competition is considered with the purchase likelihood simulation model. The part-worth utility data must be scaled appropriately for use with the purchase likelihood simulation model. The equation transforming product utility to relative purchase likelihood is as follows:

$$P_i = (100) \frac{e^{U_i}}{(1 + e^{U_i})}$$

where P_i is the purchase likelihood for product i, e is the exponential constant, and U_i is the utility for product i. That is, e^{U_i} is the same as taking the antilog of U_i, or exponentiating U_i.

One can easily perform this purchase likelihood transformation in a spreadsheet program like Excel. Assume for a given individual that the total utility for a given product is 0.75 (after adding the part-worth utilities across all the attribute levels associated with this product alternative). The purchase likelihood (using Excel formula notation) is

$$= 100 * \exp(0.75) / (1 + \exp(0.75)).$$

This formula returns 67.92, meaning that this respondent would be expected to rate this product as a 67.92 on a 100-point scale of purchase intent. Purchase likelihood predictions are averaged across respondents to reflect an average purchase likelihood for the population.

quantitative attribute See continuous attribute.

randomized design With choice-based conjoint studies, respondents can be randomly selected to receive one of many unique available questionnaires, where each one reflects design principles of level balance and independence of attributes. Given enough respondents, such randomized design plans approximate the full factorial. In other words, across many respondents every possible product configuration is presented. Randomized designs have the benefit of very good statistical efficiency, and due to the great deal of variation in the choice tasks, they control for many order, learning, and context effects.

A truly random design may be developed that draws product concepts randomly from the universe of possible product concepts, without respect to ensuring strict level balance and independence of attributes within individual respondents. Such an approach typically leads to fairly reasonable (but never optimal) design efficiency when considering pooled analysis. However, given a large enough sample, a truly random design supports relatively efficient group or aggregate analysis of main effects plus all potential interactions and cross-effects.

randomized first-choice model Also known as RFC. A market simulation model developed in the late 1990s for converting overall utility scores for competing product alternatives to probabilities of choice. Like the BTL or share of preference simulation models, it lets each individual's choice be reflected in a probabilistic manner (allows respondents to split shares among competing product alternatives). Unlike these methods, it penalizes products that are similar to others in the competitive scenario, thus reducing or eliminating IIA (red bus/blue bus) problems.

RFC is a simulation process that repeats the choice prediction for each individual (or group, if considering aggregate estimates) hundreds or even thousands of times (iterations), and averages those choices across iterations and respondents. In each iteration, random error is added to the part-worth utilities, the new product utilities are computed, and the respondent is projected to choose the alternative with the highest utility, as in the first-choice simulation model. Product alternatives that share many of the same characteristics (in terms of attribute levels) receive correlated error in each iteration and projection of choice, and therefore compete more strongly with one another. RFC acts like a tunable first-choice model, since the scaling of the shares can be made steeper or flatter depending on the variance of the added error. RFC can also incorporate a tunable amount of IIA influence (as does the standard share of preference or logit simulation model) by additionally adding independent error to each product utility sum in each iteration.

ratings-based conjoint A conjoint analysis method in which respondents use a rating scale of some sort (such as a 0 to 10 or 0 to 100 desirability or purchase likelihood scale) to indicate preference for product profiles. Examples include traditional full-profile conjoint, and graded pairs (as in ACA or pairwise concept presentation in Sawtooth Software's CVA system). However, in graded pairs, respondents use a sliding scale ranging from "strongly prefer the product alternative on the left" to "strongly prefer the product alternative on the right." Ratings-based conjoint methods have the advantage of collecting more statistical information per unit of respondent effort relative to discrete choice. However, it is argued that respondents do not rate products on some arbitrary rating scale prior to making a product choice—they simply observe competing products and directly choose.

red bus/blue bus problem See IIA.

reduced design See fractional factorial.

reliability Refers to how consistent respondents are in applying an evaluative strategy and assigning ratings or choices of product concepts. Reliability is often characterized in terms of R-squared (percent of total variation in the product ratings explained by the model) for ratings-based conjoint methods, or likelihood if considering choice-based methods.

High reliability does not necessarily lead to accurate models of real-world purchases. Respondents may answer a conjoint questionnaire very reliably, but they may not be in a realistic mindset, or the conjoint questionnaire may be seriously flawed in some way. Good reliability does not necessarily imply better data. Respondents who adopt extremely simple decision rules (such as always picking the same brand or whichever product has the lowest price) will typically receive much higher reliability scores than respondents who conscientiously consider the complex trade-offs among all attributes before making a product choice or rating.

restriction See prohibition.

revealed preference Also known as RP. A term often used by researchers with a background in econometrics to refer to predictive models built using actual store purchases or real-world choices of existing products, as well as other variables describing buyers or households. In contrast, conjoint or choice methods, based on survey data, are often called stated preference models by this same class of researchers.

reversal When an estimated part-worth utility or utility coefficient defies rational expectations or order. For example, consider the following part-worth utilities for price:

Attribute Level	Part-Worth
$10	1.50
$15	1.63
$20	0.75

We would expect that lower prices should be preferred to higher prices (all else held constant). However, the part-worths for $10 and $15 reflect a reversal—the data suggest that $15 is preferred to $10. As another example, if we fit a linear coefficient to price, we should expect a negative sign (utility is negatively correlated with price). An estimated price coefficient with a positive sign would also be considered a reversal.

Reversals are often seen within individual respondents, and are usually due to random error (lack of precision of the part-worth estimates) due to limited information. Reversals can be detrimental to individual-level predictions of behavior. But reversals due to random error at the individual level are usually of little consequence to accurate predictions of shares of preference for groups of respondents (given adequate sample size). Reversals can be eliminated by using constrained estimation. However, constrained estimation does not always improve the predictive accuracy of conjoint analysis models and therefore should be used with caution.

RFC See randomized first-choice.

saturated plan In traditional full-profile conjoint analysis, a saturated plan means that there are as many parameters to estimate (per individual) in the model as there are conjoint cards (questions). In other words, respondents are asked the bare minimum number of conjoint questions that would permit estimation of the part-worth utilities of interest. A saturated plan has no degrees of freedom, and the R-squared is always 100 percent. Therefore, it is not possible to assess respondent reliability. If respondents answer with error (which they invariably do), there is no opportunity for errors to cancel themselves out (through additional conjoint questions beyond the minimum required) or for the negative effects of these errors upon the estimated part-worth utilities to be reduced. Generally, saturated plans result in less precise (noisier) part-worths relative to design plans that incorporate additional degrees of freedom. See degrees of freedom for further discussion.

RP See revealed preference.

Sawtooth Software Privately owned software company founded by Richard M. Johnson in 1983 in Sun Valley, Idaho. Sawtooth Software's first software product was Ci2, a general Microsoft-DOS-based computerized interviewing system for computer-assisted personal interviewing (CAPI) and later computer-aided telephone interviewing (CATI). In 1985, Sawtooth Software released its first conjoint analysis package, Adaptive Conjoint Analysis (ACA). The company established a research conference starting in 1986, and papers from this conference are often cited in the literature. In 1995, Sawtooth Software moved to Sequim, Washington State.

scale factor The relative size or spread of the part-worth utilities from conjoint analysis, especially choice-based conjoint analysis. Consider the following part-worth utilities:

Respondent #1	Respondent #2
-0.5	-1.0
0.0	0.0
0.5	1.0

The difference in utility between the best and worst levels for Respondent #1 is 1.0, and the similar spread for Respondent #2 is 2.0. Respondent #2's relative scale factor is twice Respondent #1's. With logit analysis, the scale factor reflects the certainty associated with an individual's or a group's choices to the questions used in developing part-worth utilities. The scale factor also has a large impact on resulting shares of preference from the logit, randomized first-choice, or Bradley-Terry-Luce simulation methods. Respondents (or groups) with larger scale factors will have more accentuated (extreme) share predictions than those with smaller scale factors. One can change the scale factor for individuals or groups by tuning the exponent. The exponent is applied as a simple multiplicative factor to the part-worth utilities prior to predicting choice.

scenario Another term for a choice task, choice set, or set. It can also refer to a market condition tested in a market simulator. The base case is an example of a market simulation scenario.

self-explicated approach A measurement approach in which respondents are asked to directly state their preferences (utility scores) for the attributes and levels in the study. One of many such approaches has respondents rate each level of each attribute on a 10-point scale, followed by allocating 100 points across all attributes (constant sum scaling) to indicate the relative importance of each attribute. The level ratings (after normalization to reduce scale-use bias) are multiplied by the attribute importances to develop preference weights (akin to part-worth utilities) for the full set of attribute levels. Self-explicated models have the benefit of being easy to administer and able to cover a large number of attributes and levels without overburdening the respondent. But most argue that they are not very realistic, and assume that respondents can directly tell the researcher the full set of preference values.

A common mistake is to refer to these models as self-explicated conjoint. Self-explicated models are, by definition, not conjoint analysis, since they never involve asking respondents to evaluate conjoined attributes of a product. Rather, each attribute is evaluated separately. A self-explicated model is a compositional approach, and conjoint analysis is referred to as a decompositional approach.

Self-explicated models often produce quite accurate predictions of individual behavior, but typically fall short of conjoint analysis techniques in terms of predicting accurate shares of preference for market choices among available product alternatives. Of these two, predicting shares for a market is typically much more important to managers. In Adaptive Conjoint Analysis, the preliminary priors section is a rudimentary example of a self-explicated method.

sensitivity analysis In market simulations, sensitivity analysis involves changing a product specification in some way (such as increasing the price or changing the speed or color) and observing the resulting change in preference. For example, the base case share of preference for a product alternative at the middle price might be 35 percent. The researcher might lower the product's price, holding all other competitors constant, and rerun the market simulation. The new share of preference due to the lower price might then be 45 percent. By varying the product's price across all price levels, the sensitivity of the product's shares with respect to price (a relative demand curve) is estimated.

As an example of price-sensitivity analysis, here are preference shares across five prices (five separate simulation runs) for a product, holding competition constant:

Price Point	Percent Share of Preference
Low	53
Medium-Low	45
Middle	35
Medium-High	28
High	13

Often, researchers perform sensitivity analysis for a given product alternative across all levels of all attributes. The results show which attributes have the most impact on product choice, relevant to that specific product specification and the relevant competition. See market simulator.

set In discrete choice modeling or choice-based conjoint studies, "set" is often synonymous with "task" (a single choice question). In this context, a set is a collection of product alternatives from which the respondent can choose. With traditional conjoint, set may refer to the total array or deck of conjoint cards or the stimulus set.

share of preference The respondent interest captured by product alternatives in a market simulation, expressed as percentages summing to 100 percent across competing product alternatives. Share of preference represents either the percent of respondents projected to choose an alternative (assuming a first-choice simulation rule) or the average probability of respondents in the sample choosing an alternative (assuming that respondents' votes can be split in a probabilistic fashion across the product alternatives, using the logit, Bradley-Terry-Luce, or randomized first-choice rules). Practitioners use share of preference to refer to predictions from conjoint market simulators. We say "share of preference" rather than "market share" because only under controlled situations will predicted shares closely match actual market shares. See market share.

SP See stated preference.

stated preference Also known as SP or stated choice. A term often used by researchers with a background in econometrics to refer to predictive models built using the choices/ratings of product concepts made by respondents within surveys. In contrast, models built using actual sales (scanner) data or real-world choices are often called revealed preference models by this same class of researchers.

stimulus A more technical term referring to the product profile (concept) shown to respondents.

superattribute See composite factor.

task Generally refers to a single choice question (set) in a discrete choice (CBC) questionnaire. In this context, a task is a collection of product alternatives from which the respondent can choose. In full-profile conjoint, "task" can refer to the total conjoint interview. One might state, "There were eighteen total cards in the conjoint task." Task might also be used in the phrase "task complexity" to refer to the difficulty of answering an individual conjoint or discrete choice question or the entire conjoint/choice interview.

test-retest reliability Researchers sometimes repeat a conjoint question or choice task later in the questionnaire to see if respondents will answer the same way twice. The measure of how consistently respondents answer if given the same question at a later point in the survey is called test-retest reliability. When respondents choose from among three available product alternatives, research has shown that about 75 to 80 percent of respondents can answer identically in the repeated task.

Test-retest reliability establishes a benchmark for predictive accuracy. If our conjoint analysis models can only predict holdout choices with 52 percent accuracy, we should not feel the model is a failure if the test-retest reliability for the same choice tasks is only marginally better, such as 55 percent.

trade-off analysis A generic term often applied to conjoint or discrete choice analysis, emphasizing that respondents are required to trade off the benefits of attributes when evaluating product profiles, rather than being able to state that all attributes are equally important and all levels equally desirable.

trade-off matrix Also known as the two-factor method. A conjoint method developed by Richard Johnson (1974) that asked respondents to focus on just two attributes at a time using a trade-off matrix. Respondents rank-ordered, in terms of preference, all possible combinations of the two attributes. In exhibit A.10 we see a respondent who liked the blue minivan best and the red station wagon least. Respondents complete a number of these pairwise tables, covering all attributes in the study (but not all possible combinations of attributes). By observing the rank-ordered judgments across the trade-off matrices, we are able to estimate a set of preference scores and attribute importances across the entire list of attributes. As with traditional full-profile conjoint methods, utility estimation is carried out for each individual. Because the method only asks about two attributes at a time, a larger number of attributes can be studied than is generally thought prudent with full-profile conjoint methods. Trade-off matrices fell out of favor in the 1980s because Adaptive Conjoint Analysis seemed to produce better results while being less taxing on the respondent.

	Red	Green	Blue
Sedan	6	8	2
Station wagon	9	7	4
Minivan	5	3	1

Exhibit A.10. Data from a simple trade-off matrix

treatment See concept.

two-factor method See trade-off matrix.

unacceptables In Adaptive Conjoint Analysis (ACA) and other customized conjoint analysis approaches, researchers can first ask respondents (prior to asking any conjoint questions) if any attribute levels are absolutely unacceptable, no matter what other excellent qualities a product concept might have. Those levels marked unacceptable are not included in the subsequent conjoint questions, allowing the interview to focus on the relevant levels for each respondent. The unacceptable levels for a given respondent are often set to have extremely low part-worth utilities, such that a product alternative including any unacceptable level would never be chosen in market simulations.

The concept of asking respondents to discard any unacceptable levels upfront made good sense theoretically, but respondents often could not reliably indicate which levels were truly unacceptable in practice. Often, respondents would be observed to choose product concepts later in holdout tasks that included levels previously deemed unacceptable. It seems that many respondents treated the unacceptable rating as very undesirable, for which enough other good attribute levels could compensate.

Despite the challenges, unacceptables are sometimes used today. Successful applications stress very strongly to respondents that before marking a level as unacceptable, it must be absolutely unacceptable in every way, such that this level would never be chosen, even if all other included attributes were at extremely desirable levels. A recent approach for adaptive choice-based conjoint (Johnson and Orme 2007) allows a respondent to confirm that a level is unacceptable only after he or she has consistently rejected that level in many previous choice tasks.

utility An economic concept that, when used in the context of conjoint analysis, refers to a buyer's liking for (or the desirability of) a product alternative. Researchers often refer to the values for individual levels as utilities, but this is not technically correct. Utility most correctly refers to the preference for an overall product concept, whereas the components of utility associated with that product's attributes are called part-worths.

utility balance The degree to which multiple product alternatives being compared in a choice task or conjoint analysis exercise are equally matched in terms of preference. When competing product alternatives are approximately utility balanced, it requires much more thought on the part of the respondent to make a choice. More thoughtful trade-offs typically provide better information for refining part-worth utilities. However, too much utility balance can cause the trade-offs to become overly difficult, and the respondent may answer with greater randomness (noise).

vector model See ideal vector model.

version See blocking.

validity See internal validity and external validity.

volumetric conjoint A variation on the allocation-based response format for CBC questionnaires in which the values assigned to product alternatives are not required to sum to any particular value (such as 100). Rather, respondents indicate how many of each product concept they would purchase. See allocation-based response.

what-if simulator See market simulator.

Appendix B

Contributors

This book would not have been possible without the willing participation of many individuals. For contributors to chapter 13, here is the list of people and their positions at the time their case studies were submitted for publication:

Calvin Bierley. Ph.D., Marketing Statistical Analyst, Boeing Employees Credit Union.

Christopher N. Chapman. User Research Lead, Hardware Division, Microsoft Corporation.

Jim Christian. Technical Director–Market Research. General Motors Corporation.

Charles E. Cunningham. Ph.D., Professor, Department of Psychiatry and Behavioral Neurosciences, McMaster University Faculty of Health Sciences.

Margaret E. Kruk. M.D., M.P.H., Assistant Professor, Department of Health Management and Policy, University of Michigan School of Public Health.

Liana Fraenkel. M.D., M.P.H., Associate Professor of Medicine, Yale University School of Medicine.

Mike Lotti. Director, Business Research, Eastman Kodak Company.

Peter Rockers. M.P.H., Research Analyst, Center for Social Epidemiology and Population Health, University of Michigan School of Public Health.

Greg Rogers. Senior Manager, Market Research, Procter & Gamble.

Murray A. Rudd. Ph.D., Senior Economic Analyst, Department of Fisheries and Oceans, Policy and Economics Branch–Maritimes Region, Dartmouth, Nova Scotia.

Bibliography

Allenby, G. M., N. Arora, and J. L. Ginter 1995, May. Incorporating prior knowledge into the analysis of conjoint studies. *Journal of Marketing Research* 32:152–162.

Bacon, L. P., P. Lenk, K. Seryakova, and E. Veccia 2007. Making MaxDiff more informative: Statistical data fusion by way of latent variable modeling. In *Sawtooth Software Conference Proceedings*, pp. 327–344. Sequim, Wash.: Sawtooth Software.

Bakken, D. and L. Bayer 2001. Increasing the value of choice-based conjoint with "build your own" configuration questions. In *Sawtooth Software Conference Proceedings*, pp. 99–110. Sequim, Wash.: Sawtooth Software.

Chapman, C. N., J. Alford, M. Lahav, C. Johnson, and R. Weidemann 2009. CBC vs. ACBC: Comparing results with real product selection. In *Sawtooth Software Conference Proceedings*. Sequim, Wash.: Sawtooth Software. in press.

Chapman, C. N., E. Love, and J. L. Alford 2008, January. Quantitative early-phase user research methods: Hard data for initial product design. In *Proceedings of the 41st Hawaii International Conference on System Sciences (HICSS-41)*. Waikoloa, Hawaii: University of Hawaii at Manoa. in press.

Chrzan, K. 1999. Full versus partial profile choice experiments: Aggregate and disaggregate comparisons. In *Sawtooth Software Conference Proceedings*, pp. 235–25. Sequim, Wash.: Sawtooth Software.

Chrzan, K. and T. Elrod 1995. Partial profile choice experiments: A choice-based approach for handling large numbers of attributes. Presented at the American Marketing Association 1995 Advanced Research Techniques Forum.

Chrzan, K. and N. Golovashkina 2007. An empirical test of six stated importance methods. Presented at the American Marketing Association 2007 Advanced Research Techniques Forum.

Cohen, S. 2003. Maximum difference scaling: Improved measures of importance and preference for segmentation. In *Sawtooth Software Conference Proceedings*, pp. 61–74. Sequim, Wash.: Sawtooth Software.

Currim, I. S., C. B. Weinberg, and D. R. Wittink 1981, June. The design of subscription programs for a performing arts series. *Journal of Consumer Research* 8:67–75.

Finn, A. and J. J. Louviere 1992. Determining the appropriate response to evidence of public concern: The case of food safety. *Journal of Public Policy and Marketing* 11(1):12–25.

Frazier, C. and U. Jones 2004. The effect of design decisions on business decision-making. In *Sawtooth Software Conference Proceedings*, pp. 145–151. Sequim, Wash.: Sawtooth Software.

Gaskin, S., T. Evgeniou, D. Bailiff, and J. Hauser 2007. Two-stage models: Identifying non-compensatory heuristics for the consideration set then adaptive polyhedral methods within the consideration set. In *Sawtooth Software Conference Proceedings*, pp. 67–83. Sequim, Wash.: Sawtooth Software.

Gilbride, T. J. and G. Allenby 2004, Summer. A choice model with conjunctive, disjunctive, and compensatory screening rules. *Marketing Science* 23 (3):391–406.

Green, P. and V. Rao 1971, August. Conjoint measurement for quantifying judgmental data. *Journal of Marketing Research* 8:355–363.

Green, P. and V. Srinivasan 1978, October. Conjoint analysis in marketing: New development with implications for research and practice. *Journal of Marketing* 54:3–19.

Green, P. E. and Y. Wind 1975. New way to measure consumers' judgments. *Harvard Business Review* 53:107–117.

Green, P. E. and Y. Wind 1989. Courtyard by Marriott: Designing a hotel facility with consumer-based marketing models. *Interfaces* 19(1):25–47.

Gustafsson, A., A. Herrmann, and F. Huber (eds.) 2000. *Conjoint Measurement: Methods and Applications*. New York: Springer-Verlag.

Hauser, J. R., E. Dahan, M. Yee, and J. Orlin 2006. 'must have' aspects vs. tradeoff aspects in models of customer decisions. In *Sawtooth Software Conference Proceedings*, pp. 169–181. Sequim, Wash.: Sawtooth Software.

Hauser, J. R., M. Ding, and S. P. Gaskin 2009. Non-compensatory (and compensatory) models of consideration-set decisions. In *Sawtooth Software Conference Proceedings*. Sequim, Wash.: Sawtooth Software. in press.

Huber, J. 1997. What we have learned from 20 years of conjoint research: When to use self-explicated, graded pairs, full profiles or choice experiments. In *Sawtooth Software Conference Proceedings*, pp. 243–256. Sequim, Wash.: Sawtooth Software.

Huber, J. and K. Zwerina 1996, August. The importance of utility balance in efficient choice designs. *Journal of Marketing Research* 33:307–317.

Johnson, R. 1974, May. Trade-off analysis of consumer values. *Journal of Marketing Research* 11:121–127.

Johnson, R. 1987a. Accuracy of utility estimation in ACA. Technical paper available from the World Wide Web at http://www.sawtoothsoftware.com/education/techpap.shtml.

Johnson, R. 1987b. Adaptive Conjoint Analysis. In *Sawtooth Software Conference Proceedings*, pp. 253–265. Sun Valley, Idaho: Sawtooth Software.

Johnson, R. 2000. Monotonicity constraints in choice-based conjoint with hierarchical Bayes. Technical paper available from the World Wide Web at http://www.sawtoothsoftware.com/education/techpap.shtml.

Johnson, R., J. Huber, and B. Orme 2004. A second test of adaptive choice-based conjoint analysis (the surprising robustness of standard CBC designs). In *Sawtooth Software Conference Proceedings*, pp. 217–234. Sequim, Wash.: Sawtooth Software.

Johnson, R. and B. Orme 1996. How many questions should you ask in choice-based conjoint studies? Presented at the American Marketing Association 1996 Advanced Research Techniques Forum.

Johnson, R. and B. Orme 2003. Getting the most from CBC. Technical paper available from the World Wide Web at http://www.sawtoothsoftware.com/education/techpap.shtml.

Johnson, R. and B. Orme 2007. A new approach to adaptive CBC. In *Sawtooth Software Conference Proceedings*, pp. 85–109. Sequim, Wash.: Sawtooth Software.

Johnson, R., B. Orme, J. Huber, and J. Pinnell 2005. Testing adaptive choice-based conjoint designs. Presented at the Design and Innovations Conference (Berlin). Technical paper available from the World Wide Web at http://www.sawtoothsoftware.com/education/techpap.shtml.

Johnson, R., B. Orme, and J. Pinnell 2006. Simulating market preference with 'build your own' data. In *Sawtooth Software Conference Proceedings*, pp. 239–253. Sequim, Wash.: Sawtooth Software.

King, W. C., A. Hill, and B. Orme 2004. The 'importance' question in ACA: Can it be omitted? In *Sawtooth Software Conference Proceedings*, pp. 53–63. Sequim, Wash.: Sawtooth Software.

Krieger, A. M., P. E. Green, and Y. Wind 2005. Adventures in conjoint analysis: A practitioner's guide to trade-off modeling and applications. Retrieved from the World Wide Web at http://www-marketing.wharton.upenn.edu/people/faculty/green-monograph.html.

Kuhfeld, W. F., R. D. Tobias, and M. Garratt 1994. Efficient experimental design with marketing research applications. *Journal of Marketing Research* 31:545–557.

Lapin, L. L. 1993. *Statistics for Modern Business Decisions* (sixth ed.). Orlando, Fla.: Harcourt.

Levy, P. S. and S. Lemeshow 1999. *Sampling of Populations: Methods and Applications* (third ed.). New York: Wiley.

Liechty, J., V. Ramaswamy, and S. H. Cohen 2001, May. Choice menus for mass customization: An experimental approach for analyzing customer demand with an application to a Web-based information service. *Journal of Marketing Research* 38(2):183–196.

Louviere, J. and G. Woodworth 1983, November. Design and analysis of simulated consumer choice or allocation experiments. *Journal of Marketing Research* 20:350–367.

Love, E. and C. N. Chapman 2007. Issues and cases in user research for technology firms. In *Sawtooth Software Conference Proceedings*, pp. 43–50. Sequim, Wash.: Sawtooth Software.

Luce, D. and J. Tukey 1964. Simultaneous conjoint measurement: A new type of fundamental measurement. *Journal of Mathematical Psychology* 1:1–27.

McFadden, D. 1974. Conditional logit analysis of qualitative choice behavior. In P. Zarembka (ed.), *Frontiers in Econometrics*, pp. 105–142. New York: Academic Press.

Nunnally, J. C. 1967. *Psychometric Theory*. New York: McGraw-Hill.

Orme, B. 2003. Scaling multiple items: Monadic ratings vs. paired comparisons. In *Sawtooth Software Conference Proceedings*, pp. 43–59. Sequim, Wash.: Sawtooth Software.

Orme, B. 2006. Adaptive maximum difference scaling. Technical paper available from the World Wide Web at
http://www.sawtoothsoftware.com/education/techpap.shtml.

Orme, B. 2009a. MaxDiff analysis: Simple counting, individual-level logit, and HB. Unpublished working paper.

Orme, B. 2009b. Using calibration questions to obtain absolute scaling in MaxDiff. Technical paper available from the World Wide Web at
http://www.sawtoothsoftware.com/education/techpap.shtml.

Orme, B. and M. Heft 1999. Predicting actual sales with CBC: How capturing heterogeneity improves results. In *Sawtooth Software Conference Proceedings*, pp. 183–199. Sequim, Wash.: Sawtooth Software.

Orme, B. and R. Johnson 2006. External effect adjustments in conjoint analysis. Technical paper available from the World Wide Web at
http://www.sawtoothsoftware.com/education/techpap.shtml.

Orme, B. and R. Johnson 2008. Testing adaptive CBC: Shorter questionnaires and BYO vs. "most likelies". Technical paper available from the World Wide Web at
http://www.sawtoothsoftware.com/education/techpap.shtml.

Orme, B. and W. C. King 1998. Conducting full-profile conjoint analysis over the Internet. Technical paper available from the World Wide Web at http://www.sawtoothsoftware.com/education/techpap.shtml.

Orme, B. and J. Loke 2005. Personal communication. Unpublished research at Sawtooth Software.

Otter, T. 2007. Hierarchical Bayesian analysis for multi-format adaptive CBC. In *Sawtooth Software Conference Proceedings*, pp. 111–126. Sequim, Wash.: Sawtooth Software.

Page, G. and J. Raymond 2006. Cognitive neuroscience, marketing and research. Presented at the 2006 ESOMAR Congress.

Pinnell, J. 1994. Multistage conjoint methods to measure price sensitivity. Presented at the American Marketing Association 1994 Advanced Research Techniques Forum.

Pinnell, J. 1999. Should choice researchers always use 'pick one' respondent tasks? In *Sawtooth Software Conference Proceedings*, pp. 207–223. Sequim, Wash.: Sawtooth Software.

Renkin, T. G., G. Rogers, and J. Huber 2004. A comparison of conjoint and scanner-data-based price elasticity estimates. Presented at the American Marketing Association 2004 Advanced Research Techniques Forum.

Rice, J. and D. Bakken 2006. Estimating attribute level utilities from "design your own product" data—chapter 3. In *Sawtooth Software Conference Proceedings*, pp. 229–238. Sequim, Wash.: Sawtooth Software.

Sawtooth Software 1993. Choice-based conjoint analysis. Technical paper available from the World Wide Web at
http://www.sawtoothsoftware.com/education/techpap.shtml.

Sawtooth Software 2008, Fall. Update on computer usage survey. Retrieved from the World Wide Web at
http://www.sawtoothsoftware.com/education/ss/ss29.shtml.

Sawtooth Software 2009. Laptop computer study. Online demonstration available from the World Wide Web at
http://www.sawtoothsoftware.com/test/byo/byologn.htm.

Snedecor, G. W. and W. G. Cochran 1989. *Statistical Methods* (eighth ed.). Ames, Iowa: Iowa State University Press.

Srinivasan, V. and A. D. Shocker 1973. Linear programming techniques for multidimensional analysis of preferences. *Psychometrika* 38:337–369.

Stevens, S. S. 1946. On the theory of scales of measurement. *Science* 103: 677–680.

Vriens, M., J. Huber, and D. Wittink 1997. The commercial use of conjoint in North America and Europe: Preferences, choices, and self-explicated data. Unpublished working paper.

Williams, P. and D. Kilroy 2000. Calibrating price in ACA: The ACA price effect and how to manage it. In *Sawtooth Software Conference Proceedings*, pp. 81–95. Sawtooth Software.

Index

A

ACA, *see* conjoint method, Adaptive Conjoint Analysis

ACBC, *see* conjoint method, adaptive choice-based conjoint

adaptive choice-based conjoint, *see* conjoint method, adaptive choice-based conjoint

additive model, *see* model type

additivity, *see* model type, additive model

aggregation, *see* limitation

allocation, *see* conjoint task, allocation

alternative-specific attribute, *see* attribute

attribute, 7
  alternative-specific, 33
  compound, 41
  constant, 33
  definition, 51–56
  level, 51–56
  list, 51
  multimedia, 52
  must-have, 118, 121
  mutually exclusive, 53
  number-of-levels effect, 54, 55
  prohibition, 55, 56, 79

attribute importance, *see* measure, importance

B

best-worst scaling, *see* maximum difference scaling

binary attribute, *see* measure, binary

binary data, *see* measure, binary

Bradley-Terry-Luce model, *see* simulator

brand equity, *see* business application and measure

BTL model, *see* simulator, Bradley-Terry-Luce model

business application, vii, 31, 32, 35, 127–139
  brand equity, 22–24
  education, 134–136
  environmental protection, 133, 134
  financial services, 132, 133
  forecasting, 93–95, 128
  health care, 129, 130, 134–136
  line extension, 98
  manufacturing, 128–131
  pricing research, 24, 25, 84–88, 92, 95–98, 127–129, 136, 139
  product design, 4, 92–95, 98–101, 128, 129
  segmentation, 26, 47, 65, 90–92, 98–101, 134

C

cannibalism, *see* measure, cross-elasticity

card-sort conjoint, *see* conjoint task

categorical variable, *see* measure, nominal

CBC, *see* conjoint method, choice-based conjoint

chip allocation, *see* conjoint task

choice, *see* conjoint task

choice simulator, *see* simulator

cluster analysis, *see* statistics

compound attribute, *see* attribute

concept, 2

concept test, 1, 4

conjoint method
  adaptive choice-based conjoint, 49, 117–126
  Adaptive Conjoint Analysis, 4, 32–34, 42–44, 46, 49–51, 53, 56, 63, 86, 130
  choice-based conjoint, 4, 20, 22, 33–35, 45–50, 52, 64, 65, 79, 80, 128, 129
  full-profile conjoint, 8, 30, 31, 33–35, 39, 41, 46, 50, 63, 64

conjoint simulator, *see* simulator

conjoint task
  allocation, 45
  card-sort, 2, 30, 41, 53
  choice, 5, 20–22, 33, 45, 46
  holdout, 16, 17, 47, 62
  pairs, 20, 21, 41, 44
  ranking, 30, 31, 43, 46
  rating, 3, 30, 43, 46
  trade-off matrix, 31

constant attribute, *see* attribute

207

S

sales forecasting, *see* business application, forecasting
sample size, *see* statistics
sampling error, *see* statistics
SAS, *see* software, Statistical Analysis System (SAS)
SAS Institute, *see* software, Statistical Analysis System (SAS)
Sawtooth Software, *see* software
scale use bias, *see* response style
segmentation, *see* business application
self-explicated task, 19, 20, 42–44
sensitivity analysis, 81–84, 95
share, *see* market share or measure, share of preference
share of preference, *see* measure
share of preference prediction, *see* market share or measure, share of preference
simulation method, *see* simulator
simulator, 3, 4, 11, 26, 32, 35, 36, 48, 52, 53, 55, 81, 84, 88–103
 Bradley-Terry-Luce model, 90, 102
 first-choice model, 90
 logit model, 90, 102
 multi-store, 103
 randomized first-choice model, 90
software, 32, 36, 131
 Bretton-Clark Software, 32
 Microsoft Excel, 67, 69–74
 Sawtooth Software, ix, 20, 32, 34, 39, 41, 42, 44–46, 63, 64, 127, 128
 Statistical Analysis System (SAS), 35, 39
 Statistical Package for the Social Sciences (SPSS), 39

SPSS, *see* software, Statistical Package for the Social Sciences (SPSS)
Statistical Analysis System, *see* software
Statistical Package for the Social Sciences, *see* software
statistics
 cluster analysis, 98
 confidence interval, 59–61
 finite population correction, 61, 62
 log-log regression, 97
 margin of error, 59–61
 measurement error, 58, 62–65
 regression analysis, 31, 73, 74
 sample size, 57–66, 102
 sampling, 48
 sampling error, 58
 standard error, 59, 60

T

trade-off matrix, *see* conjoint task
traditional conjoint, *see* conjoint method, full-profile conjoint
treatment, *see* concept

U

utility, *see* measure, part-worth
utility balance, 118

V

virtual shopping, 35

W

willingness to pay, *see* measure